The BEST OF HANCOCK

Written by
Ray Galton and Alan Simpson

Drawings by John Ireland

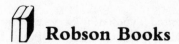 Robson Books

First published in the United Kingdom in 1986 by Robson Books Ltd, Bolsover House, 5–6 Clipstone Street, London W1P 7EB.

Copyright © 1986 Ray Galton & Alan Simpson

British Library Cataloguing in Publication Data

Galton, Ray
   The best of Hancock.
   1. Hancock's Half Hour (Television program)
   I. Title   II. Simpson, Alan, 1929–
   791.45'7   PN1992.77.H/

   ISBN 0-86051-367-X

Typeset by Computerised Typesetting Services, Finchley, London.
Printed in Great Britain by The Garden City Press, Letchworth.

Contents

Introduction

WE FIRST MET Tony Hancock in the stalls of the Paris Cinema in October 1951, during rehearsals of a radio show starring Derek Roy, in which he was appearing and to which we were contributing, albeit not the bit in which he was appearing. Is that clear so far? We didn't say anything to him and he didn't say anything to us. Thus began a partnership that lasted until 1961 and encompassed 103 radio half hours, 65 television half hours, 26 other assorted radio shows, 1 film, 2 stage shows and several Workers' Playtimes, Variety Ahoys, Music Halls, etc. All in ten years. Just think what we could have achieved had we spoken to each other that afternoon! Let that be a lesson to all married couples — or married triplets in this case.

For the historically minded (if you're not you can skip this bit and rejoin us at the beginning of the next paragraph), the scripts collected here were all written between 1959 and 1961, and have been issued on video cassette prior to their being repeated on television in 1986, together with eight other shows not included here. The BBC have only thirty-seven of the original sixty-five television shows left in the archives and we recently had the difficult task of selecting eighteen out of these for the initial series of repeats. Certain old favourites, some of which are in this collection, picked themselves, but in the end it was a toss-up which to include, and there remain at least twelve tapes that will make a very good series of repeats in the future.

Welcome back to those readers who skipped the preceding paragraph. Some of you will find it interesting to have the scripts on your lap, or perhaps on somebody else's lap, while playing the videos. In the privacy of your own home you could pretend to be Duncan Wood, the director, and call out instructions to the artists and see if they take any notice of them. This is best done behind locked doors or when everybody else has gone out. Or better still, you could join the local branch of the TONY HANCOCK APPRECIATION SOCIETY, where your condition would go completely unnoticed.

If you do compare the scripts with the videos, you will find that the performances are virtually word perfect, not as common as you might think in comedy shows. On occasions, however, you will come across cuts in the text. These were either made at the first read-through, during rehearsal, or edited out after the performance, and always because of time. We were generous writers. We always gave the BBC more than they paid for. We cannot remember a script of ours that was written exactly to time. We estimate that an average of three minutes per script had to be cut out at some stage of production. Not a lot, you may think, but if you multiply that by the 168 Hancock's Half Hours written, you come up with the conclusion that the equivalent of sixteen half hours have been written and never seen. A statistic that still brings tears to the eyes of our agent.

Finally, we hope you will get many hours of enjoyment from these scripts. They're fairly easy to read, you won't need to refer to a dictionary, at least not as often as we had to whilst writing them. And if you do find yourself getting bored half-way through, you can always go down to your public library and borrow *Lady Don't Fall Backwards.* You never know, their copy might have the last page in it.

RAY GALTON AND ALAN SIMPSON

The Economy Drive

First transmitted on 25 September 1959

The Economy Drive featured
SIDNEY JAMES
with
PATRICIA HAYES
LIZ FRASER
PAMELA MANSON
MICHAEL WARD
PEGGYANN CLIFFORD
TOTTIE TRUMAN TAYLOR
ARTHUR MULLARD
ALEC BREGONZI
LAURIE WEBB
HERBERT NELSON
FRANK PEMBERTON
ANNE MARRYOTT
MARIO FABRIZI

Produced by DUNCAN WOOD

SCENE 1   Outside No. 23, Railway Cuttings. Piled up high, covering the whole doorstep, and spilling over on to the pavement, is about three months' supply of full milk bottles. Inside the house, behind the front door, is three months' delivery of newspapers, letters, etc. piled four feet high on the mat.

   After a few seconds there is a tremendous clatter as the milk bottles get knocked over outside. Tony and Sidney have arrived back home. They are dressed in Slavonic national costume — baggy trousers, Magyar shirts, embroidered hats.

Tony: You great oaf! I thought I told you to cancel the milk.

Sidney: Oh, shut up moaning. Open the door.

Tony: Four hundred bottles of milk — look at it. What am I going to do with four hundred bottles of milk?

Sidney: Take it in and have a bath.

Tony: Very funny. Come on, help me up. (*Grunts and groans as he gets up*) You know you're supposed to cancel the milk when you go away on holiday. It's a dead give-away for burglars, that is. I bet there's not a stick of furniture left in there.

Sidney: Oh, for crying out loud, open the door! This case is heavy, let's get in. I've been listening to you moaning through eighteen countries, now give it a rest.

Tony: (*mumbles to himself*) Well, all that milk on the step, right down to the gutter it is, they all know we've been away. It's all very well for you, there's nothing of yours in there, a dead lumber, some people. . . (*Trails away into silence*)

Sidney: (*pause*) Now what's wrong?

Tony: I can't find the door key.

Sidney: It's hanging on the string behind the letter-box.

Tony: Oh, you're joking, aren't you? You haven't left it hanging behind the door?

Sidney: Yeah.

Tony: Oh well, we've had it, haven't we? I doubt if there'll be any wallpaper left. When I think I've spent three miserable months galloping round the Continent with my key hanging behind the front door — Well, I'm not going in. All my

heirlooms and my objets d'art bundled up in some masked gentleman's sack —
why didn't you just pin a note on the door, 'Gone away for three months, come
in and help yourself'? What a buffoon you are! Do you think I'm made of
money? Mind out of the way.

(*The letter-box opens and Tony's hand comes through. The hand pokes around feeling
for the key dangling on a bit of string. He finds it and pulls it up through the letter-box.
The key goes in the lock and the door opens but is stopped by the papers and letters piled
up behind it. There is just room for Tony's foot to get round the door*)

Sidney: Well, come on, open it.

Tony: I can't open it. There's something on the other side. (*Sudden thought*) It's a
burglar! He's hiding behind there . . . waiting for us. I can see him! (*He has his
face pressed up against the frosted glass on the door. Behind the door is a hatstand with a
bowler hat and an overcoat on it*) He's got a bowler hat on! It's Raffles, the
gentleman crook! Give yourself up, open the door and come out with your
hands up —

Sidney: Come out of it . . . (*He forces the door and comes into the hallway. He looks
around and sees the hatstand. He is disgusted*) Raffles!

(*Tony pokes his head round the door, frightened. He looks around*)

Tony: Has he gone? (*Sidney just points at the hatstand. Tony sees it*) Oh, Oh yes.
Well, it could have been. There was no point in taking chances. (*He drags his cases
in, puts them down and closes the front door. He then sees the pile of papers behind the
door*) What's all this, then?

Sidney: I didn't cancel the newspapers, either.

Tony: Oh, Sid — why don't you think of me for a change? I've got to pay for all
these.

Sidney: Well, they're only twopence halfpenny each.

Tony: I have five a day. Seven days a week. And they're dearer on Sunday. Plus
your *Greyhound Gazette* . . . And there's my *Health and Beauty*, that's one-and-
six, and there's twelve of those, and my *Farming News*, the *Ballroom Dancing
Weekly* and *Film Fun*. There's about twenty-three pounds' worth of out-of-date
literature there.

Sidney: All right, I'm sorry. We'll cut your losses. I'll take it all down the fish
shop in the morning, see what I can get on them. (*He bends down and starts sorting
the letters from the papers*)

Tony: (*hanging up his hat*)A penny a pound they'll give you. I'll be lucky to get a
tanner back on that lot. And all that milk gone to waste — sixteen pounds ten of
bottled cheese out there. And I've got to go out and buy a new suit in the
morning. I can't turn up at the BBC in this. If they see me dressed like this they'll
have me in *Balalaika* before I can look round.

Sidney: (*still sorting*) It's not my fault.

Tony: It *is* your fault. If you hadn't got mixed up with those two Yugoslavian
wine treaders it would never have happened. (*Mimics*) 'Wouldn't it be funny if
we wore each other's clothes for an evening?' Never saw them again. They
knew when they were on to a good thing. The toast of Belgrade, those two are
now. Jumping around inside a barrel of grapes with my Savile Row flare-line on
— it's not good enough. I felt a right Charlie coming through the customs in this
lot. Look at us! We look like refugees from *The Chocolate Soldier*.

Sidney: (*wearily*) Don't keep on, there's a good boy.

Tony: I have every right to keep on. I don't know how I'm going to make ends meet. And with you wasting all this money needlessly — I don't mind telling you, Sid, I'm worried sick.

Sidney: Oh, cor blimey, I don't understand you people. What's the point of worrying about money? Eat, drink and be merry, for tomorrow we snuff it. You know my philosophy: if you've got it, spend it, if you haven't got it, get it.

Tony: Oh, you Fatalist, you. You've spent too much time in the East, that's your trouble. Come on, let's get unpacked.

(*They go into the living-room. Immediately Tony sees the light is on. It is a chandelier, with all lights blazing*)

Tony: Three months that's been blazing away!

Sidney: I left it on purposely. With the light on the burglars would have thought there was somebody here, so they don't come in.

Tony: (*angry*) Twelve bulbs left on, twelve of them! It would have been cheaper if they *had* got in. At least they might have switched the lights out when they left. (*Switches light off*) Do you think I'm made of money? This waste has got to stop, Sid.

Voice: (*distorted from TV set*) Good evening. Welcome to another evening's television.

(*Tony freezes*)

Sidney: That's funny, I thought I switched that off. Never mind, we won't have to wait for it to warm up now, will we. (*Goes to sit down in front of the set*)

(*Tony rushes over to switch it off. He yells and shakes his hand*)

Tony: It's red hot! Me tube's gone, it must have.

Sidney: It hasn't gone, there's nothing wrong with it.

Tony: Listen, mate, that smoke's not coming from *Gun Law*. Look at the glue holding the set together!

Sidney: Where?

Tony: There, oozing out and running down the sides. Take a week to cool down, that will. What a fool you are! Fancy leaving a television set on for three months. Three months! Twenty-four Bilkos have been flashing round this room with no one to look at them. Well, you can buy the next set, I'm not. I'm going upstairs to change. (*Going away*) How can a man be so absent-minded? I've never come across a more inconsiderate, thoughtless, wasteful. . .

(*He shuts the door behind him. Sidney immediately rushes over and switches off the electric fire and pulls the plug out. He rushes over to a table on which stand unwashed breakfast things. He pulls the plug out of the electric toaster and takes from it two completely black bits of bread which burn his fingers. Quickly he throws them out of the wide open window and closes it, just as Tony comes back in. Sidney goes all nonchalant as if nothing has happened*)

Tony: All right, come on, what was it?

Sidney: What was what?

Tony: What did you just switch off?

Sidney: Nothing.

Tony: Yes, it was. I went to have a look at the meter to see how much electricity we've burnt. That little flat disc inside was hurtling round like a Catherine wheel. Then it suddenly slowed down. What was it? What did you switch off?

Sidney: Oh, all right, then. It was the electric fire.

Tony: The electric fire? How many bars?

Sidney: All of them.

Tony: Three bars . . . a penny a bar an hour . . . for three months. What my electricity bill for the quarter is going to be I hesitate to think. Do you realize you didn't switch off one thing in this house? Not one thing. The washing machine was still on. All the water's evaporated and what's happened to the shirts I don't know. All I could hear were six buttons and a collar stud rattling around. It's probably ruined it. I'll have to phone for the man to come round and look at it now. (*He goes over to the phone and picks it up. He rattles the receiver up and down*)

Sidney: You won't get anything out of that.

Tony: Why not?

Sidney: (*dead pleased*) I had it cut off before we left. You see, I didn't forget everything, did I?

Tony: (*replaces the receiver*) You had it cut off? The one thing in the house you can leave on without it costing anything, you have cut off. *And* you have to pay to have it put back on again. I wouldn't mind betting you left the car running in the back garden.

Sidney: Oh dear. . .

Tony: Oh, no!

Sidney: I can't remember.

Tony: (*horrified*) My car! Seized up! My 1927 Green Label Bentley lying out there with six rigid pistons! (*He rushes to the back door and opens it. About two hundred assorted loaves of bread fall in on top of him*) That's it. That is it! (*He picks up a cottage loaf in one hand and a very long French loaf in the other hand, holding them like an orb and sceptre*) Would you care to explain this?

Sidney: When's the coronation? (*Laughs*)

Tony: (*slings the bread down in disgust*) This is the last straw! I distinctly told you to cancel the bread. Look at it all. (*Bangs the table with one solid loaf*) Solid. No wonder the place hasn't been burgled — they couldn't get in. What are we going to do with this lot?

Sidney: You could build a garage for your rigid Bentley.

Tony: It's nothing to laugh at. This is sheer extravagant waste, and I can't afford it any more. I haven't got much money as it is, by the time I've paid for all this lot (*waves his hands round the room*) I'll be flat broke. Well, we are cutting down. As from today we are starting an economy drive.

Sidney: (*worried*) What do you mean?

Tony: Aha, now you're worried, it's going to hurt you, isn't it? We've had our holiday, we are now going to make a fresh start. We have got to live to the absolute minimum until I am solvent again. No more waste, no more luxuries, austerity is going to be the motto in this establishment. And when we eat out, no more posh restaurants. The Dorchester is out. From now on, nothing over three bob.

Sidney: You can't do that! A man in your position, you've got appearances to keep up. You can't let the public see you queuing up with a tray at the Corner

House. And what about your business lunches? All those big producers?

Tony: That is a fallacy. If they want you, they're not going to worry about where they eat.

Sidney: Well, I can't see J. Arthur Rank leaning up against a pie stall with a contract in one hand and a sausage in the other.

Tony: It doesn't have to be a pie stall. There are other places where one can eat quite reasonably. We've got to cut down on our expenditure and that is that. As that immortal character Mr Micawber said to Oliver Copperfield in *Bleak House* by Monica Dickens, 'Oliver,' he said (*W.C. Fields' voice*) 'A bit of advice, my boy, a bit of advice.' (*Own voice*) I only saw the film. 'Annual income twenty pounds, annual expenditure nineteen pounds nineteen and sixpence, result, happiness. Annual income twenty pounds, annual expenditure twenty pounds and sixpence, result, misery.' So in future I shall live within my means, starting as from lunch-time today.

Sidney: You going out to eat now?

Tony: I am.

Sidney: It's a bit early, isn't it?

Tony: Yes, well, I intend to call in at the Railway Lost Property Office first to buy a suit. You can make your own arrangements. I shall see you after lunch, and don't turn anything on.

Sidney: All right, all right.

Tony: I've read the meter. Just one therm and you're out, mate. Good day to you.

(*He goes out. There is the sound of the front door opening and slamming. Then a terrific clatter of milk bottles as he falls over them again. Sidney reacts despairingly*)

SCENE 2
A self-service cafeteria (a replica of Lyons). The place is very busy and noisy. There is a counter with the usual metal pigeon-holes containing the dishes. A cashier sits at the end of the counter. There is a queue, all holding trays with food on.

Tony creeps in with dark glasses on to avoid recognition. He now has on plus fours, a flat cap and golf shoes. He looks round surreptitiously, trying to keep his face averted from the crowd. He sees people taking trays and joining the queue. He goes up to the trays, looks round and reaches for a tray. As he does so, a waitress comes along and bangs another pile of trays on top of his hand. He reacts in mute agony, pulls his hand out and wriggles the fingers. He looks round and goes to get a tray with the other hand. A second waitress bangs another pile of trays down on it. He reacts in mute agony again.

He recovers, and goes to take another tray. This time the first counter girl is standing by ready to bang a pile of trays on top of the main pile. Tony pauses and watches her. She watches him. Tony indicates 'After you'. She indicates 'After you'. Tony insists she goes first. She insists he goes first. Finally they both do it at the same time and he gets his hands caught under the pile again.

A man comes up and takes a tray and is about to walk past Tony when Tony snatches the tray from him, indicating that he was here first. The man takes another tray and moves in behind Tony in the queue. The queue moves off on the long trek to the counter. The queue makes two U-turns before reaching the counter. The man is holding his tray out in front of him and pushes Tony in the small of the back. Tony in his turn pushes the man in front of him and this goes on down the line. They all turn round and glare at Tony. Tony protests it wasn't him but the man behind.

They continue queuing and the man again pushes Tony in the back with his tray. The same chain reaction results and all turn and glare at Tony again. Tony, after protesting his innocence, grabs the man and shoves him in front of him. They move off again, and the chap now behind Tony pushes him in the back with his tray, producing the chain reaction once more. Tony quickly pushes the bloke behind him in front of him before the others turn round and glare. So they now glare at the man Tony has pushed in his place. Tony has a go at him as well.

The queue moves on and Tony finally reaches the counter. He puts his tray on the tray runner. He takes his knife and fork from the box on the counter. Holds the knife up to see if it's clean. He looks for a handkerchief but hasn't got one, so takes the first man's handkerchief out of his top pocket and cleans his knife. During this business the queue behind him have pushed their trays along the counter, taking Tony's tray with them. They push past Tony to keep up with their own trays, so that when Tony has finished cleaning his knife and goes to put it on his tray, he finds it's not there. He looks round, then sees his empty tray halfway up the counter with six people and their trays between him and it.

Tony: Excuse me, my tray.
(*The man in front of him bars his way and won't let him past*)
1st Man: Do you mind, this is a queue.
Tony: Yes, but my tray has been pushed up there.
1st Man: Well, that's hard luck, because you're not getting in front of me.
(*Tony doesn't quite know what to do. Finally he takes a roll from under the glass container, measures the distance between him and his tray and lobs the roll up the queue, trying to land it on his tray.*

Meanwhile his tray is getting closer to the cashier as the other members of the queue take their food from the little compartments and push further on, taking Tony's tray with them. Tony takes a trifle off the counter and measures up the distance, but thinks better of it, puts it back, and pushes frantically past the people in front of him to reach his tray. They protest and try to stop him but he manages to get past. He reaches his tray just as it reaches the end of the counter so that he is now in front of the cashier with his empty tray)
Cashier: (*surveys the tray*) What's the matter, are you on a diet?
Tony: Well, as a matter of fact. . .
Cashier: Haven't we got anything you like?
Tony: Well, it's not that, you see. . .

Cashier: Look, we haven't got time for your little jokes, it's the rush hour. (*She tots up the next man's tray*) Shilling, one-and-six, two-and-three, two-and-nine, three-and-five, four-and-twopence, four-and-eightpence-halfpenny.

(*The man hands her his money. She rings it up. Tony tries to push his way back down the queue, but they bar his way*)

Cashier: Do you mind moving away, you're creating a disturbance.

Tony: I'm trying to get back to fill my tray up.

Cashier: You'll have to go out that way and back.

(*Tony sets off outside the rail that borders the queue back to the point where the food counter starts. He then tries to duck under the rail to get in the queue. A man objects*)

2nd Man: Oi — what are you trying to do?

Tony: I've queued up once, I didn't quite manage to get any food on my tray. You see, I've never been in one of these places before, I'm not used to the technique. . .

2nd Man: Well, you're not coming in here.

(*Tony tries to get in a little further down*)

3rd Man: You're not coming in here, either.

Tony: But I've already queued up once.

3rd Man: That's your hard luck — you'll have to queue up again, won't you.

Tony: But I'm just trying to get in my rightful place.

3rd Man: I don't like queue jumpers — now, hoppit.

(*Tony goes up to a woman who has reached the hot dish section in the middle of the counter*)

Tony: Excuse me, madam, would you mind passing over an Individual Fruit Flan?

Woman: Are you speaking to me?

Tony: I've got a better idea, do you mind if I stand next to you?

Woman: I beg your pardon?

Tony: I'll just slide in, no one will notice. . .

(*He bends down to get under the rail*)

Woman: How dare you — keep away from me, keep away — I'm being molested — where's the manager? Get the manager, I'm being molested!

Tony: (*getting up from under the rail*) Don't bother, I'm just going. . . (*To the crowd*) The woman's a fool. . .

4th Man: Is he annoying you, lady?

Woman: He tried to get in next to me.

Tony: I was only after an Individual Fruit Flan.

Woman: Call the manager.

Tony: Oh, shut up. (*He stalks off*) Oh, these foreign art students are all the same. . .

(*As he passes the queue on his way to the back he exchanges threatening gestures with them. He joins the end of the queue. The queue moves up again. He once again reaches the counter. He is in a terrible mood. He picks up some cutlery and slings it on his tray. He pushes the tray along to the roll and butter place. He picks up a roll, presses it, and puts it back*)

1st Girl: (*smoking a cigarette behind the counter*) You've handled that, you've got to have it now.

Tony: I don't want it, it's hard.

1st Girl: You've handled it — this is a hygienic establishment, I can't pass that on to somebody else. . .

Tony: Oh, all right. (*Puts it on his plate*) And two pats of butter . . . no, one pat of butter . . . no — er — one pat of margarine.

1st Girl: This is a self-service establishment.

Tony: Then what are you doing behind the counter?

1st Girl: Replenishing.

Tony: Well, replenish those rolls then. Like hand grenades, they are.

(*He moves his tray along to the compartments with the hot dishes in*)

Tony: (*to the man behind him*) It's like *Take Your Pick* this, isn't it? (*Laughs. To girl along the counter*) I'll have the key to Box Thirteen, please. (*Laughs.*) (*They all just stare at him stonily. He dries up, and busies himself lifting the flaps of the metal compartments to see what's inside them. They are empty. He calls to the girl*)

Tony: Oi, Miss!

(*She walks along the counter and disappears behind the compartments. She is now opposite Tony with the compartments between them, so that he cannot see her*)

2nd Girl: What do you want?

(*Not being able to see her, Tony starts lifting up the flaps to find her. The compartments are simply shelves so that when you lift up a flap you can see right through to behind the counter. Finally he lifts up a flap and the girl is the other side looking through at him*)

Tony: Oh, there you are. What about replenishing some of these?

2nd Girl: All those that are empty are off. There's a mince and baked beans here.

(*Her hand comes out of one of the flaps holding a plate of mince and baked beans*)

Tony: (*disgusted*) I don't want that.

2nd Girl: Did you handle it?

Tony: Certainly not. That's the last thing I'd handle, mince and beans.

2nd Girl: What's wrong with it?

Tony: I just don't like mince and beans. I can't ever recall a time when I have liked mince and beans. I'm just not a mince and beans man. That's all there is to it. You could call it an unreasonable hatred if you like, but there it is, that's the way I'm built. What else is there?

(*The hand goes in and another one comes out with another plate much higher up the compartments*)

Tony: You're jumping about a bit behind there, aren't you? How tall are you?

2nd Girl: My friend is helping me. Meat patty and beans, do you want it?

Tony: No, I don't. What other delicacies do you keep hidden away from the public gaze?

(*Three hands come out of various compartments holding plates. Tony looks at them in turn*)

Tony: No, there's nothing there — everybody in! Haven't you got any plaice and chips?

2nd Girl: Second from the end, middle row.

(*Tony starts counting the compartments. Gets confused and starts again. The man behind him goes straight to the right compartment, takes out a plaice and chips, and puts it on his tray*)

Tony: Just a minute, that's mine!

5th Man: How do you make that out? First come first served, mate.

Tony: Well, I was first.

5th Man: Not to that compartment, you weren't. Excuse me. (*Tries to push past Tony, who bars his way*)

Tony: That is my plaice and chips. You wouldn't have known where it was if I hadn't asked.

5th Man: Don't be ridiculous — I come here every day, I know where they keep the plaice and chips. Excuse me.

(*He pushes past and carries on. Tony lifts up the flap on the plaice and chips compartment. The girl's face is the other side, staring at him. By now Tony is the only one at the counter*)

2nd Girl: Yes?

Tony: I want another plaice and chips, please.

2nd Girl: Sorry, that was the last one. Have a meat loaf and peas.

Tony: (*grimaces*) Oh, cor. . .

2nd Girl: Top left-hand corner.

Tony: Oh, very well. (*He takes a plate from the top left-hand corner compartment*) Revolting. (*He puts it on his tray and moves down the counter towards the cashier. On his way he takes a sweet from the sweet section. He reaches the tea girl who is the last one before the cashier*) Tea, please. Not much milk and a slice of lemon.

Tea Girl: No lemon and the milk's already in.

(*She pours him a cup from the urn and hands it to him. He puts it on the tray and moves on to the cashier*)

Cashier: One-and-nine, two-and-three, three-and-two. Four-and-fivepence, please.

Tony: Four-and-fivepence? For this load of rubbish?

Cashier: You've got the dearest hot dish there and the dearest sweet. Four-and-fivepence, please.

Tony: I'm sorry, I'm on an economy drive, I am only allowed three shillings a day for dinner.

Cashier: I can't help that, what you've got on that tray is four-and-fivepence.

Tony: I haven't got four-and-fivepence, I only brought the exact three shillings, to avoid temptation.

Cashier: Then you'd better change your selection, hadn't you?

Tony: I was hoping to get ten cigarettes out of my three shillings, as well. I thought these places were cheap. Good grief, woman, this is sheer extortion.

Cashier: Four-and-fivepence, please, or change your food.

Tony: Very well, I shall change it.

(*He goes back to the hot dish compartment. Puts the plate back in the top left-hand compartment. On the other side of the counter, we see a plate come out the other side of the compartment and fall to the ground. The girl behind the counter comes up*)

2nd Girl: Who did that? Who did that?

Tony: I was only putting it back where I got it from.

2nd girl: There was another one in there.

Tony: It was empty just now.

2nd Girl: I replenished it. One plate, one drawer. You can't put two plates in.

Well, I'm not paying for it. (*Calls to the cashier*) Edie, charge this gentleman for one meat loaf and peas.

Tony: Very well, but you will not have the benefit of my custom again, young lady. In future I shall take my tray elsewhere.

(*He goes back to the cashier*)

Cashier: It's still four-and-fivepence.

Tony: And I've still only got three shillings, and I'm hungry.

Cashier: Well, I'm sorry, the meat loaf and peas is two-and-six, and you've got to pay for it. You'll have sixpence left. And there's one-and-eleven on the tray. You'd better take the sweet and tea back. That'll leave you fivepence to pay. You'll have a penny change, then.

Tony: Oh good, I can have another pat of margarine.

Cashier: Put the sweet and tea back. (*Tony does so*) That's it. Two-and-eleven, please.

Tony: Two-and-eleven — for a roll and marge! The one part of the meal you get for nothing at the Dorchester. A big basketful, as many as you like. Shout out 'Encore du pain' and they're up with another load. Give us my penny.

(*He takes a tureen lid and puts it over his roll to keep it warm. He takes up his tray with the roll and marge on it and looks for a seat. He finds one with the woman he 'molested' sitting at it with her back to him. He goes to sit down and she sees him*)

Woman: Ooooooh. . .!

Tony: Oh, cor. . .!

(*He rises again and hastily looks for another table. He finds one and sits down. He takes his roll and marge and places it on the table. He gets up to put his tray on the pile of used trays. As he puts it on, the waitress bangs another pile of trays on his fingers. He reacts. Goes back to the table. He sits down in front of his roll and marge, unfolds a table napkin and tucks it in his collar. He cuts the roll open and butters it. Puts salt and pepper inside it. The first waitress passes*)

Tony: Have you got any salad cream, please? (*She hands him a bottle of salad cream. He pours some on to the roll, then some tomato sauce on to the plate*) Ah, that's better, I'm going to enjoy this. (*The plate is swimming in salad cream, etc. He picks up a knife and fork, then thinks better of it. He turns round to the table behind him*) Excuse me, could you pass that spoon over?

(*Second waitress comes along with a trolley, collecting the dirty things. She picks up his plate and scrapes his roll and marge into a waste bin and moves on. The people on the other table find Tony a spoon and pass it to him. He turns back with spoon poised to start, and sees his plate has gone. He turns and looks suspiciously at the man next to him, who is eating away quite unconcerned. They are the only two at the table. The man becomes conscious of Tony's stare and glances at him. Tony moves the man's plates about, looking for his roll and marge. He can't find it*)

Tony: All right, where is it?

Man: Where's what?

Tony: My roll and marge and salad cream and sauce.

Man: (*revolted*) You don't think *I* would eat it, do you?

Tony: Two-and-eleven that cost me, mush – what have you done with it?

Man: I haven't seen it.

Tony: You must have seen it. It was a roll with loads of margarine on it, floating

in a sea of tomato sauce and salad cream.

(*The man winces, pushes his dinner away, gets up and leaves*)

Tony: (*calls after him*)I say — you haven't finished your soup! You haven't even started your entrée. What a peculiar man. Oh well, waste not, want not. (*He lifts the cover off the man's dinner*) Mince and beans! (*Disgusted, he gets up and stalks out*)

SCENE 3 Tony's living-room. The chandelier has only one bulb in it. Tony and Sidney are sitting by the fire in their overcoats. Sidney has a big tartan rug wrapped round his legs. He is freezing cold. Tony is rolling a cigarette in a machine. Signs are hung round the room: 'Close that door', 'A closed door means a warm room', 'Turn that light out', 'Waste not, want not', 'A thrifty man is a happy man'.

Tony: Where's my box of filters?

(*He takes them from the table. He puts three filters in the machine, then a little tobacco. He inserts a cigarette paper, rolls it in, licks the end. He finishes rolling it in. He takes the cigarette out, puts it in his mouth, and it comes unstuck*)

Sidney: Why don't you buy some cigarettes?

Tony: It's cheaper this way. Four hundred for one-and-nine.

Sidney: You haven't made one yet. Three ounces of tobacco you've wasted.

Tony: I've saved on the matches, though.

(*He starts again. Sidney shifts uncomfortably in his chair. While Tony is occupied, Sidney tries very craftily to put another piece of coal on the fire with the tongs. The fire consists of a big grate with one piece of coal in it. Just as Sidney is about to drop the piece of coal on, Tony spots him*)

Tony: Ah ah ah ah! Put it back.

Sidney: But it's freezing in here.

Tony: Put it back. One lump every hour. We've had our ration for tonight. I'll be going up to bed in fifteen minutes' time. Save the lights.

Sidney: But it's only seven o'clock.

Tony: If you think I'm going to sit down here with that thing burning away all night, you're mistaken. Forty watts, that is. If we go to bed now we'll save fourpence on that. (*He has licked the end of his cigarette paper. He takes the cigarette out and it comes unstuck again*) Oh, I think I'll give it up.

Sidney: What a miserable existence this is. You might as well be dead. (*Starts pacing up and down*) No fire, no telly, no fags, nothing to eat, nothing to drink, go to bed as soon as it gets dark, get up as soon as it gets light, don't put the lights on, don't put the fire on, don't turn the tap on, watered-down milk (*Sidney gradually gets worked up. Tony just sits and stares at him*), stale bread — it's worse than prison. I can't stand it much longer, do you hear? I can't stand it much longer — halfpenny here, penny there, can't have this, can't have that, don't do this, don't do that — I can't live like this, do you understand, I can't live like this, it's driving me mad, mad, mad, MAD.

Tony: Don't walk up and down, it wears the carpet out.

Sidney: What's it all for, tell me that? How much have you saved?

Tony: You mind your own business. Suffice for you to know I'm quite happy with the way things are going. (*He picks up a cash box and rattles it.*) Three weeks' economizing, that is. I reckon another five years of this and we can afford to ease up a bit.

Sidney: Five years! Cor blimey. . .

Tony: Well, bed now. Come on . . . and no reading up in your room.

Sidney: What — with a meter — a shilling for five minutes — that's right.

(*Tony tucks his box under his arm. They reach the door. Tony switches the light off. They go out into the hall. It is pitch black*)

Tony: Come on, up the stairs.

(*The rest of the scene is played in pitch darkness*)

Sidney: Oh, for crying out loud, surely we can have a light on till we get up there?

Tony: We don't need a light just to climb up a dozen stairs — what's the matter with you?

Sidney: I can't see where I'm going.

Tony: What do you think banisters are for? Honestly, you make things hard for yourself, you do. Go on, there's another two steps. Or is it three?

(*Terrific crashes and bangs and yells as they fall downstairs*)

SCENE 4 A hospital ward. Tony and Sidney are in adjacent beds. Tony has his leg up in plaster. Sidney also has a leg up in plaster, and his head swathed in bandages. Tony is having his dinner.

Sidney: (*disgusted*) Economizing! (*Mimics Tony*) 'We don't need a light just to climb a dozen stairs.'

Tony: I cannot be held responsible for your great plates going through holes in the carpet.

Sidney: Get some new carpets.

Tony: Carpets cost money. You don't half moan, don't you? I'm not worried. Apart from the pain and the agony, I'm quite happy. Four weeks we'll be in here. Four weeks of luxurious living without costing a penny. That's the way to economize. The Welfare State's going to take a bashing with my meals, I can tell you. Marvellous. (*He finishes his last mouthful and rings a bell*) More, more. Seconds . . . More. . .

(*Sidney looks at him in disgust and turns over*)

SCENE 5 The hospital almoner's desk, which displays a notice saying 'LADY ALMONER'. She is working. Sidney and Tony enter in their street clothes. Both have sticks. They hobble over to the desk. Tony points to the notice and reacts, impressed.

Tony: (to Sidney) Lady Almoner. (To the lady almoner) Good afternoon, your ladyship. Very nice to see the aristocracy helping out at the local hospital.

Almoner: (confused) Oh . . . yes . . . can I help you?

Tony: Just off. Hancock and James, Emily Trubshawe Ward. We've had a very pleasant stay here — very nice hospital you run. I'm sure Lord Almoner must be very proud of you. Good day to you.

Almoner: Just a moment — Mr Hancock and Mr James?

Tony: That is correct.

(The lady almoner looks through some papers)

Almoner: Ah, here we are. (She hands Tony two sheets of paper) Your bills.

Tony: I beg your pardon?

Almoner: Your bills, for your hospital treatment.

Tony: No, no, madam, we're National Health. We're not on this private caper.

Almoner: I'm sorry, I'm afraid you are. I looked into the matter and I find you're out of benefit. Your insurance cards haven't been stamped for over three months. That'll be fifty guineas each, please.

Sidney: Fifty guin — (To Tony) You were stamping the health cards.

Tony: I was economizing. I mean, eleven-and-three a week's a lot of money and we were healthy lads, it seemed a waste of money.

Sidney: Well, I'm not paying, it's your responsibility. . .

Almoner: That'll be a hundred guineas then, please, Mr Hancock. We'll take a cheque.

Tony: Yes, I expect you would . . . Not from me though, girl. All the money I've got in the world is in here . . . (Rattles his box)

Sidney: Serves you right. (Snatches the box, tips a pile of money on to her desk) Here you are, missis, pick the bones out of that. If there's any over, give it to the nurses.

Tony: Ruined! All that scrimping and scraping for nothing.

Sidney: It's not that bad. You paid all your bills off, and you've been away from home for four weeks, no electricity, no fires . . . You haven't got any money, but at least you don't owe anybody anything.

Tony: That's true. I suppose things could be worse. Come on, let's go home and have a drink.

Sidney: That's more like it. Switch the fire on as well, shall we?

Tony: Why not? Only one bar, of course.

Sidney: All right, then.

(They go out happily)

SCENE 6
The hallway of Tony's house. As in Scene 1, it is packed with newspapers. A hand comes through the letter-box, grabs the piece of string with the key on it. The door opens, revealing Tony and Sidney standing on the porch chest high in milk bottles. Tony just looks at Sidney.

Sidney: Well, I had a broken leg — I couldn't cancel them. I was in agony . . . the last person I thought of was the milkman. (*Pause*) Well, I don't suppose there's all that much bread round the back door. We weren't away for so long this time.

(*Tony picks up a bottle and surveys Sidney, weighing up the merits of bashing him with it*)

Sidney: A little bit of economy, we'll soon pay this lot off. (*Pause*) Well, I'll be off then.

(*A voice is heard: 'This is BBC Television' followed by Charlie Drake saying 'Hello, my darlings'. Tony comes into action. He tries to bash Sidney with the milk bottle. Sidney makes off. Tony throws the bottle down the road after him. Then he picks up more milk bottles and hurls them after Sidney, one after another*)

The Two Murderers

First transmitted on 2 October 1959

***The Two Murderers* featured**
SIDNEY JAMES
with
ROBERT DORNING
PATRICIA HAYES
HUGH LLOYD
RALPH NOSSEK
MARK SINGLETON
ARTHUR MULLARD
TOM CLEGG

Produced by DUNCAN WOOD

SCENE 1 Tony's living-room. Tony enters carrying a tin cash box.

Tony: Sid! Sid! Are you in? Sid? (*Waits for answer. Silence.*) Good, he's out. (*He puts the cash box on the table, locks the door, pulls the blind down and draws the curtains across it. He goes over to the table, puts a green eye-shade on, and gets the full bank set out — scales, shovel, sponge pad, cash bags, etc. He opens the box and empties a pile of money on to the table — notes and coins. He gives a miserly chuckle and runs his fingers through it*) Aha, mine, all mine. My life's savings. Look at all that snow there. (*Chuckles*) Very comforting. I've got enough here to buy everything I want in the world, but I'm not going to because I'd sooner have the money. Right, lads, eyes down for the annual count-up. (*Gets stuck into the counting. Puts elastic bands round the bundles of notes. Singing as he does it, he shovels the coins into cash bags, weighs them and does them up. He comes across a pound note.*) Hallo, a blue pound note. I've had you a long time, mate. You were called in years ago. Nohap, you're still legal tender, in you go. (*Drops it in the box*) Well, well, a silver threepenny bit! Dear oh dear, you've seen the inside of many a pudding, haven't you, mate? I remember digging you out — Christmas, nineteen thirty-eight, round me Auntie Beat's. Ah dear me, there's some memories amongst this lot. There's some old favourites here. The three pennies I had thrown at me during the Royal Command Performance. Very embarrassing, that was. Especially when everybody saw where they came from. Still, there we are, threepence is threepence. (*There is a banging on the door. Tony immediately with a reflex action covers his hoard with his arms*) Who is it?

Sidney: It's me — Sid.

(*Tony is worried. Sidney bangs on the door again, then tries the door handle*)

Sidney: What are you doing in there? Let me in.

(*Tony jumps into action. He quickly sweeps all the money into the cash box, locks it, puts all the bank equipment away, and rushes over to the fireplace. Hanging down the chimney is a rope with a hook on the end. He hangs the cash box on the hook, and pulls what seems to be the curtain sash for drawing the curtains together. As he pulls, the box disappears up the chimney. He then draws the curtains manually and lets the blind up*)

Sidney: (*banging on the door*) Hurry up, what's going on in there?

(*Tony tiptoes over to the door and unlocks it. He runs over to the couch and sits down nonchalantly*)

Tony: Come.

(*Sidney comes in, looking suspiciously around*)

Sidney: Did you have a bird in here?

Tony: That was a very cruel remark if ever I've heard one. You are fully aware of my lack of success with the ladies. There hasn't been a bird in here since Dolly Clackett got married. I shall never forgive her. On the very Saturday when I lashed out — to please her, mark you — one hundred and twenty pounds on an Italian Scooter and two skid lids . . . And you talk about having birds in here — I wouldn't give them house-room.

Sidney: You had the curtains drawn.

Tony: Yes . . . well . . . you know how sensitive I am. I just don't like people looking in.

Sidney: You were counting your money, weren't you?

Tony: I was not.

Sidney: Don't give me that old codswallop. You were counting your money. It's your annual count-up.

Tony: I haven't got any money. I'm a very poor man.

Sidney: You've got a fortune stacked away here somewhere. I just don't know where you keep it, that's all.

Tony: And you won't find out, either.

Sidney: Oh, so you admit it?

Tony: I don't admit anything.

Sidney: All right, have it your own way. But listen to me, I have got the hottest business proposition to put to you that has come my way in years.

Tony: No.

Sidney: You haven't even heard it yet!

Tony: I don't care, not a penny.

Sidney: But this is a racing certainty.

Tony: They always are.

Sidney: Never like this, never like this. This is the chance of a lifetime. A genuine, straightforward, one hundred per cent honest business investment. It can't miss. Are you interested?

Tony: No.

Sidney: You fool — you short-sighted fool. You've always been telling me to get an honest business, and this is it. Let me tell you about it. I have made a takeover bid for the most successful shop in Cheam High Street.

Tony: Not the undertakers?

Sidney: No, no. All right then, the second most successful. Mabel's Fish and Chip Parlour.

Tony: Mabel's Fish and Chip Parlour? Successful? She hasn't got through that bundle of newspapers I sold her last year yet.

Sidney: No, you've got it wrong, she's making a bomb. I've seen the books.

Tony: She's cooked them, and that's the only thing she is cooking, believe me.

Sidney: All right, that doesn't matter, it's the ideas I've got for it. I've got plans. I'm going to do it up like a coffee bar. I'm having the whole shop done out like an underwater cavern. Tables shaped like big oyster shells . . . seaweed hanging up the walls . . . fishing nets, plastic shrimps hanging from the ceiling, and waitresses done up like mermaids, hopping round the tables, see. . .

Tony: And I suppose you'll have me sitting in a big chair with a long beard holding a trident.

Sidney: I'll clean up! Plate of fish and chips, bread and butter and a pickled onion, four-and-a-tanner. It could be a household name in Cheam . . . El Fish and Chipo. Look, whoever goes into this with me is going to make a small fortune, and I am giving you first refusal.

Tony: All right, then, I refuse.

Sidney: Please, Hancock, please, I'm serious about this. I've put everything I've got into it, but I need some more capital.

Tony: I'm sorry, Sid, I see nothing but disaster in this scheme. Save your money, because you're not getting any of mine.

Sidney: That's your last word?

Tony: That is my last word.

Sidney: You selfish swine! You know how much this means to me and you won't lift a finger to help me. I'll remember this, Hancock. You let me down in my hour of need.

Tony: Oh, don't go maudlin.

Sidney: (standing) All right — but you won't stop me. I'll get that money, don't you worry. There's other ways of getting hold of it.

Tony: What do you mean by that?

Sidney: (at the door) Never you mind. You've had your chance. If you won't give it to me, I'll get it another way.

(Sidney leaves. Tony is worried. He goes over to the curtain sash and lowers the cash box. He unhooks it, and looks around, biting his lip. He creeps out into the hallway. He twiddles the finial on the bottom banister post as if it is a safe combination: two turns to the right, three to the left. He lifts up a stair. The carpet is cut across and comes up with it. He puts the cash box inside the stair, lowers the step and fiddles with the finial again. He smirks at his cunning)

SCENE 2 A bank manager's office. Sidney is sitting opposite the Manager, who is writing.

Manager: Well, Mr James, I think this sounds like a very good investment. The bank will be only too happy to oblige. I've arranged for you to have an overdraft of two thousand five hundred. We're always willing to assist our customers with solid business propositions like the El Fish and Chipo.

Sidney: Thank you very much. I don't know why blokes bother to come in here with masks and guns when you can get it like this.

Manager: Well, we prefer to do business this way of course. (Laughs)

Sidney: (laughs with him) Well, I'll let you have the deeds of the place as soon as the deal is completed.

(They both rise and shake hands)

Manager: Well, then, Mr James, may I wish you the very best of luck in your new venture.

Sidney: Thanks very much. You've been most helpful.

Manager: Good afternoon.

(He ushers Sidney out)

SCENE 3   The library. A couple of people are having their books stamped by the male librarian. Sidney comes from amongst the bookshelves carrying two books. He takes them up to the desk, and hands them to the librarian.

Sidney: I'll have these two, please, Harry.

Librarian: Oh, hallo, Sid. (*Looks at the books Sidney has chosen*) *Successful Shopkeeping* and *The Art of Catering* — this is a bit out of your usual line, isn't it, Sid?

Sidney: Yeah, well, I'm opening a business. Thought I'd better read up on the whys and wherefores.

Librarian: (*stamping the books*) I've just remembered, Sid, I've got a book here that'll interest you. Right up your street. You like crime books don't you?

Sidney: Yeah. What is it — a whodunnit?

Librarian: No, this is all true stuff. All unsolved murders. Look. (*Takes a book from under the desk*) *Perfect murders of the Twentieth Century.* Very good, it is. All the old dears are taking it out.

Sidney: Yeah, all right, then, I'll give it a flip through.

    (*The librarian stamps it and hands it to Sidney*)

Librarian: Chapter Eighteen's a lovely one. Beautiful murder, blood all over the place, marvellous bit of work it was.

Sidney: (*not very interested*) Yeah? If you get any more books on business and stuff, keep 'em by for me, won't you. See you. . .

SCENE 4   Tony's living-room. Sidney is engrossed in *Perfect Murders of the Twentieth Century*. Tony comes in.

Tony: Oh . . . hallo.

Sidney: (*engrossed in the book*) Hallo.

    (*Tony sits down. There is an awkward silence for a few moments*)

Tony: How are you, then?

Sidney: (*without looking up*) I'm all right.

Tony: Oh, good. (*Pause*) You're — er — you're not still annoyed because I wouldn't lend you the money, then?

Sidney: No, no, that's all right. I told you I'd get the money, one way or another.

Tony: So you're quite happy, then?

Sidney: Oh yes, yes, I'm quite happy. I've got it all worked out.

Tony: Where are you going to get the money, then?

Sidney: Here and there, dodging around. I've got my methods.

Tony: Yes . . . yes, of course. I mean, you understand why I couldn't see my way clear to lending you the money?

Sidney: Of course, that's all right. Don't think anything more of it.

Tony: What are you reading?

Sidney: Oh . . . a book I got out of the library.

Tony: (*pause*) You're not holding it against me, then?

Sidney: No, no. I quite understand. (*He closes the book, puts it down and gets up. He yawns*) Well, I'm going up to bed. Goodnight.

Tony: Goodnight.

Tony: (*as Sidney reaches the door*) We're still friends, then?

Sidney: Yeah, of course we are.

Tony: You appreciate my position . . . I mean, it was a lot of money you wanted and after all. . .

Sidney: Forget about it. I'll get the money. (*He shuts the door*)

Tony: I don't like it. He's far too happy about it. He shouldn't be this complacent about not getting my money. He should be dead shattered. He's up to something. 'I've got it all worked out,' he said. 'I've got my methods,' he said. What did he mean by that? He doesn't know anybody else with money, and he's still going through with it. He's been far too nice with me . . . He's plotting something. I don't like it at all . . . What's he going to do? (*By now he is pacing up and down,. He stops by Sidney's chair and idly picks up the book Sidney was reading. He freezes as he sees the title*) Perfect Murders of the Twentieth Century. (*Horror*) He's going to do me in! I knew he was up to something! No . . . No, he wouldn't do a thing like that, not Sid. He wouldn't murder me for a fish and chip shop. Not his best friend. It's ridiculous. I mean more to him than a few bits of rock salmon. Pull yourself together, you imaginative fool . . . (*Idly flicks over the pages*) No, you've got to have a much bigger reason for doing somebody in than a tatty old fish and chip shop. (*Reads*) 'Chapter Eighteen. This is an extraordinary case in which a man murdered his best friend for the sake of a ten shilling note.' (*He reacts with a terrified expression*) A ten shilling note! And he's after two and a half thousand! 'I'll get the money one way or another,' he said. This is like something out of Agatha Christie. Ten Little Indians, and I'm all ten of them. Oh, this is too fantastic for words, my imagination's running away with me — Sid murdering me — how absurd can you get? What are the facts, what are the facts? Sid's set his heart on a fish and chip shop, he wants me to give him the money, I won't give it to him, and he's reading about perfect murders. Do you think that's enough evidence? Do you really think that's enough evidence? Well, it's good enough for me, mate, I'm off.

(*He rushes to the door, and Sidney is standing there in a very dramatic light. His appearance should make the audience jump as well as Tony, who practically faints away*)

Sidney: What's the matter with you?

Tony: Oh . . . I . . . what were you standing there for?

(*Sidney comes in the room. He is in pyjamas and dressing-gown*)

Sidney: I just came down to lock the doors.

Tony: What are you going to lock the doors for?

Sidney: I always lock the doors.

Tony: Yes, but why are you locking them tonight?

Sidney: For the same reason as I lock them every night — to stop people getting in. What's the matter with you?

(*He goes towards the door leading to the back. Tony jumps in his path*)

Tony: I've locked the back door.

Sidney: Oh. Well, I'll lock the windows up then.

(*He goes to the windows and pulls the latches. As he moves around, Tony places himself so his back is never turned to Sidney*)

Sidney: Well, that's that. Are you going to bed?

Tony: Er . . . yes. No. Why, what do you want to know for?

Sidney: I just wondered whether you were going to bed or stopping down here all night.

Tony: You want me to go to bed, is that it?

Sidney: Well, yes, I don't want you clumping around down here all night, I want to get some sleep.

Tony: I see. You want me in bed and fast asleep, no doubt.

Sidney: Well, it's night-time, isn't it?

Tony: It's easier when people are asleep, isn't it?

Sidney: What is? What are you talking about?

Tony: I've decided, I shall be stopping down here.

Sidney: All right, then, stop down here. I don't care, good luck to you.

Tony: Oh, you'd *like* me to stop down here, then? So that's your game.

Sidney: I don't care if you stop down here or go up to bed, or what you do, as long as you don't make a noise.

Tony: Oh, I'll make a noise, don't you worry. The whole neighbourhood will hear.

Sidney: Are you feeling all right? (*He feels Tony's forehead*)

Tony: (*breaking away from him*) I'm perfectly well, thank you . . . at the moment. I have changed my mind, I shall go up to bed. I'm not stopping down here with you roaming about the house. And I'm bolting the door to my room.

Sidney: (*utterly confused by all this*) You can board up the windows for all I care, I just want to get some kip.

Tony: After you.

(*Sidney goes out of the room, watched carefully by Tony who follows, taking a huge metal ornament for protection*)

SCENE 5
Sidney's and Tony's bedrooms. They have a centre dividing wall so both bedrooms can be seen at once. The two doors are at the back of the set, one on each side of the dividing wall. They open the doors to their rooms at the same time. Tony backs into his room)

Sidney: (*at the door*) Goodnight.

Tony: Goodnight.

(*They close the doors. Tony stands by his. After a short pause he looks out down the corridor then closes his door and locks it. Meanwhile Sidney has taken off his dressing-gown and climbed into bed. Tony tucks his pillows under the bedclothes to make it look like a body. He then puts a chair facing the door, takes his blunderbuss out of the dresser and sits on the chair at the ready. He switches out the light which is on the wall next to him*)

Sidney: (*sitting up in bed*) He's behaving very strangely. I wonder what's got into him. That strange look in his eye — he frightened the life out of me. I wonder what he's up to? I'll have to watch him. (*Yawns, settles down. Sits up*) I haven't had my corned beef sandwich. Blimey, I can't go to sleep without my corned beef sandwich. Fancy forgetting that. (*Gets up, puts his dressing-gown on. He goes out of his room, slamming the door*)

(*In Tony's room the light instantly goes on. He cocks his gun at the ready. Nothing happens. He creeps over to the door and unlocks it. He opens it and peers out down the corridor*)

Tony: I knew it, he's started! He's gone to find a weapon. No . . . my money! Of course — he's looking for the money before he does it. He wants to make sure it's going to be worthwhile. Well, we'll soon see about that. (*He creeps out of the room*)

SCENE 6
The kitchen. Sidney is trying to cut a loaf of bread. The knife is blunt and won't cut, so he starts sharpening it on one of those butcher's sharpening steels. The knife is an evil-looking bread knife.

Tony creeps along the hallway from the foot of the stairs. He reaches the door to the kitchen, and looks through the crack. He sees Sidney sharpening the knife and testing the edge. The bread is not visible. Tony looks horrified.

Tony: Oh no! (*Puts his hand to his throat*) Not the knife! What a way to go — twelve-and-a-half inches of cold Sheffield right across your tonsils. The fiend! The cold-blooded fiend! What's his next move? When's he going to do it? The book — of course — he's working to the book. (*He rushes into the living-room, grabs the book and starts frantically thumbing through it*) X, X one, X one one, X one one one, X one vee — oh, these Roman numerals — where's Chapter Eighteen? Ah . . . 'He crept into his friend's bedroom, and while the poor unsuspecting wretch was fast asleep he plunged the bread knife through the sheets down to the hilt . . . eighteen times . . . and then with a mad frenzy' — wait a minute, this is Chapter Seventeen. Thank goodness for that, I didn't fancy the mad frenzy one little bit. I'll have to tear this chapter out in case he changes his mind. Chapter Eighteen, that's the one he was reading . . . ah . . . this one also crept into his friend's bedroom. . .

(*Meanwhile Sidney has come out of the kitchen holding a huge sandwich, which he is chewing happily. Just as he gets to the foot of the stairs he notices the light is on in the living-room)*

Sidney: That's funny. He said he was going to bed. I knew he was up to something. (*He creeps over to the door and pushes it open and listens to Tony reading*)

Tony: '. . . and while his friend was fast asleep, he crept into the room, stood over him, pulled the trigger and let loose the contents of his double-barrelled shotgun into the inert body.' Yes, that's the way it'll be done. (*He fingers the gun he is still carrying*)

    (*Sidney drops his sandwich to the floor in horror. He is dead scared*)

Sidney: He's going to do me in! He's off his rocker — what does he want to do me in for — his best friend? I've never done anything to him. No, what am I thinking about, he couldn't do a thing like that, not old Hancock. He wouldn't hurt a fly. He's got no reason to get rid of me. I haven't got anything he would want. Yes, I have. Of course! He's after my fish and chip shop. He knows it's going to be a little gold mine. That's why he wouldn't lend me the money, he wants to get it for himself! He's money mad. The swine! The cold-blooded swine! Protection — I've got to protect myself.

    (*He nips back into the kitchen to get the bread knife*)

Tony: Well, he's not getting me without a fight.(*He opens the door, blunderbuss at the ready, and goes upstairs*)

Sidney: (*coming into the hall from the kitchen with the bread knife*) Well — if he tries anything, I'm ready for him.(*He goes upstairs*)

    (*In their respective bedrooms they prepare to spend the night on guard, each sitting on an upright chair and clutching his weapon. They turn out their lights*)

SCENE 7   **The living-room next morning. Sidney comes in backwards with a towel over his shoulder, brandishing his knife. He backs across the room and out of a door leading to the bathroom. The door from the passage opens and Mrs Crevatte comes in carrying a loaded shopping basket. She starts unloading it.**

Mrs Crevatte: I don't suppose those two lazy so-and-so's are up yet. Oh, I'm turning this job in. It's that fat one, he's the cunning one. 'Only for a week,' he said, 'while I'm ill.' Five years ago, that was.(*She takes out of her basket a tin of weedkiller. It is clearly marked 'POISON' in large letters, with a skull and crossbones on the label. She puts it on the mantelpiece*) I'd better tell him I've got his weed-killer for him. I'll leave it for him to put away, I'm not touching it. Oh, well, I suppose I'd better go and get their breakfast. (*Goes out, muttering*) I'm turning it in next week, I'm giving my notice in, it's not worth it for four-and-six a week. I'll tell him straight . . . (*She closes the door behing her*)

    (*There is a pause. The door opens and Tony comes in with his dressing-gown on and a towel slung over his shoulder. He is carrying his gun. He backs into the room just as*

Sidney enters from the other door. They circle round each other warily, both on their guard, watching for the slightest move. Finally they slide into their chairs on either side of the breakfast table. Tony puts his gun on the table, with the barrel pointing at Sidney. Sidney lays his knife down within easy reach. They eye each other warily. Mrs Crevatte comes in with the breakfast. She lays the plates in front of them. They don't look at her but keep watching each other)

Mrs Crevatte: Where's all the knives gone?

Sidney: *(startled)* Gone — where — where?

Mrs Crevatte: They were in the kitchen yesterday, but they've gone. There's not a knife left in the house.

Sidney: All right, Hancock, where's the knives?

Tony: *(guiltily)* Knives? What knives? I'm not telling you . . . that is, I don't know. I've sold them . . . I've sent them away to be cleaned — er — sharpened — er — new handles put on them.

Mrs Crevatte: *(throws some spoons on the table)* Well, you'll just have to use spoons.

Sidney: You can't eat egg and bacon with spoons.

Mrs Crevatte: Well, it's either that or your fingers.*(She leaves)*

Sidney: Well, I'm not bothered, I've got a knife.

(He starts cutting up his bacon with the bread knife and a spoon. Tony starts trying to cut his breakfast up with two spoons. He fails after a bit of a struggle)

Tony: Oh, this is useless. Lend us your knife.

Sidney: You're joking!

Tony: Oh come on, I can't cut my breakfast up.

Sidney: Give us your gun first.

Tony: What for? You can't eat your breakfast with a gun.

Sidney: You're not having my knife unless I have your gun. I'll swop you.

Tony: *(weighs it up)* Oh, very well.

(They hand each other their weapons. But both are reluctant to let go of their own weapon. They start tugging slightly. Finally they let go and the weapons are changed over. Tony cuts his breakfast up. They now eat their breakfast in silence, eyeing each other while we hear what each is thinking)

Tony: *(thinks)* I wonder why I didn't notice his eyes before. Real murderer's eyes — look at them. Cold, ruthless, cunning. The eyes of a killer. Homicidal maniac written all over his face. When I think of how long I've known him, I go cold. He's evil. Dead evil. I saw the way he cut that bacon up. Very professional. You can't use a knife like that and be normal. I don't think he knows I suspect him, I've been acting very normally.

Sidney: *(thinks)* What's he looking at me for? He's got that look again. He's mad — look at his eyes — shifty. I've never noticed it before, but I can see it now. A born killer. He enjoys it, he likes killing people, you can see it in his face. He's gloating over me. Relishing it. He can't wait to see my lifeless body spread out all over the floor. And I always thought he was harmless. I don't think he knows I suspect him, I've been playing it pretty cool.

Tony: *(thinks)* He's staring at me again. He loathes me. Look at those hands — look at the strength in them. Strangler's hands, they are. I can feel them round my throat, choking me, squeezing the life out of me.*(He involuntarily holds his throat and twitches his mouth)*

Sidney: (*thinks*) Hallo, he's started twitching. They always twitch. Just let him make one move and I'll have him. (*He reaches for the gun*)

Tony: (*thinks*) He's going for the gun. (*Reaches for the knife*) Go on then, one move and I'll have you.

(*After a few moments they both relax their grip on their weapons*)

Tony: (*thinks*) He's just remembered — he can't do it while Mrs Crevatte's here.

Sidney: (*thinks*) He's changed his mind. He's going to wait till Mrs Crevatte's gone.

Tony: (*thinks*) I didn't reckon on him shooting me. According to the book, he's going to knife me. What's it to be — knife or gun? The cunning fiend. (*He looks round and freezes with horror at the sight of the tin of poison on the mantelpiece*) Poison! He's going to poison me! Twisted up on the floor with my tongue hanging out of my cakehole — the most horrible way of all. He's a monster — a cold-blooded monster. That wasn't there last night. He's been out and bought it this morning. (*Sudden thought*) Perhaps he's already done it. (*Turns his breakfast over with the spoon*) I thought that egg tasted a bit off. (*Clutches his stomach*) I've been poisoned! I can feel it just starting to work. A doctor! I must get to a doctor!

(*He jumps up, and to Sidney's astonishment rushes to the door*)

Tony: (*aloud*) You monster, you black-hearted monster!

Sidney: It's a trick. What's he up to now? Where's he gone? He wouldn't go before he'd done me in. (*Gets up and sees the poison. Picks it up. Freezes*) He's already done it! He's poisoned me! (*Clutches his stomach*) That's why he's gone,

he's already done it. That egg — of course! The egg, I thought it tasted funny,
I'm dying. I'm dying. A doctor. I must find a doctor!
  (*Sidney rushes out of the room*)

SCENE 8 Two doctors' surgeries, divided by a screen. Tony and Sidney rush into their respective surgeries at the same time.

Both together: Doctor, I've been poisoned!
Tony: I haven't got long. You've got to work fast. It's probably a rare South
  American poison unknown to medical science.
Sidney: (*clutching his stomach*) It's just here. It's burning me insides out. I'm dying.
Tony's Doctor: Sit down Mr Hancock, I'll examine you.
Sidney's Doctor: Relax, Mr James, I'll have a look at you.
  (*The two doctors then carry out the identical examination: they look at their tongues,
  peer into their eyes, feel under their arms, press their stomachs, take their pulses*)
Tony's Doctor: There's nothing wrong with you. You're imagining things.
Tony: But the pain!
Tony's Doctor: You're eating too much. Go on a diet. I'll give you some pills.
  (*Starts writing*)
Sidney's Doctor: I can't find anything wrong with you, you're as fit as a fiddle.
Sidney: But I'ver been poisoned! I can feel it burning . . . right here.

Sidney's Doctor: You've been drinking too much. I'll give you a tonic. (*He starts writing*)

Tony: You're wasting your time, pills aren't going to do any good. I am being poisoned, mush.

Tony's Doctor: (*annoyed*) You are not being poisoned.

Tony: That's what they said to Mrs Crippen.

Tony's Doctor: Will you kindly stop wasting my time. (*He tears off the prescription and hands it to Tony*) There you are.

Tony: Very well, but I may as well warn you, I am coming off your register. Another doctor will have the benefit of my eleven-and-fourpence a week. I am going to get another opinion. (*He stalks out*)

(*Sidney's doctor finishes writing*)

Sidney's Doctor: (*handing prescription to Sidney*) There you are.

Sidney: (*looking at the prescription*) A bottle of red stuff? That's no good to me. I want some anti-weed-killer injections.

Sidney's Doctor: There's nothing wrong with you, now will you kindly leave my surgery?

Sidney: (*going to the door*) You haven't heard the last of this. I'm going to get another opinion.

Sidney's Doctor: By all means, please do. (*He starts writing*)

(*Sidney enters Tony's doctor's surgery and Tony enters Sidney's doctor's surgery*)

Both together: Doctor, I've been poisoned!

(*The two doctors assume expressions of weariness*)

SCENE 9   Sidney's and Tony's bedrooms as before. Sidney is asleep with the knife across his chest. Tony is asleep with the gun across his chest. The alarm bell rings. They wake up. Tony starts feeling himself all over.

Tony: (*with relief*) Cor . . . thank goodness, I'm all right. No blood, good. I'm all here.

(*They get up. Suddenly they each see a letter on the floor that has been slipped under their respective doors. They bend down and pick them up*)

Tony: (*opening his letter*) Hallo. 'Dear Hancock, I can't stand this any longer. You can have my fish and chip shop, but please don't murder me.'

Sidney: (*reading his letter*) 'Dear Sid, my life means more to me than my money, you can have every penny I've got if you promise not to do me in.'

(*They both react on reading the letters, then they both turn and rush to the doors. Sidney gets there first and bursts into Tony's room, waving the letter*)

Sidney: What are you talking about?

Tony: What are you accusing me of?

Sidney: I thought you were trying to murder me.

Tony: I thought you were trying to murder *me*.

Sidney: Me? Murder you? What for?

Tony: You wanted my money.

Sidney: No, no, you were going to murder *me*, you were after my fish shop.

Tony: I was not, how dare you! Hancocks never run fish shops. It was you who was after my money.

Sidney: I don't need your money. I've got an overdraft from the bank.

Tony: You mean you weren't going to murder me, then?

Sidney: Of course I wasn't going to murder you.

Tony: But I thought you were . . . and you thought I was . . . We've been a couple of Charlies on the quiet, haven't we?

Sidney: Well, cor blimey, fancy us not trusting each other, after all these years . . .

Tony: How long is it — ten, fifteen years? I apologise, Sid, I really do.

Sidney: How do you think I feel? I should have known you wouldn't do a thing like that . . .

Tony: Well, and you, one of the nicest fellows who ever drew breath.

Sidney: Well, well, well, all this for nothing. I've been frightened out of my life.

Tony: Well, I'm twenty years older . . . (*Shows Sidney his hair*) Look. Another three days and it would have gone.

Sidney: Well, what about some breakfast?

Tony: Good idea.

> (*They leave, Sidney with his arm round Tony's shoulders*)

Tony: I can't get over it, Sid. I mean, fancy me thinking that you. . .

SCENE 10 The living-room. Two bruisers are sitting at the breakfast table. Tony and Sidney enter, arms round each other.

Tony: I mean, you of all people, my oldest friend. Morning.

1st Bruiser: Morning.

Sidney: Morning.

2nd Bruiser: Morning.

Sidney: (*to Tony*) Who's that? (*Nodding at 1st Bruiser*)

Tony: Oh him, he's a . . . he's a . . . a very old friend of the family, came to stay a few days with us. Who's that? (*Nodding at 2nd Bruiser*)

Sidney: Oh, he's a cousin of mine, I invited him down for a week or two.

> (*They sit down. Mrs Crevatte comes in with the breakfast and sets it down*)

Tony: Fancy you thinking I was going to poison you, eh?

Sidney: Yeah, and you thinking I was trying to poison you.

Tony: Well, I'm ashamed, I really am.

Sidney: So am I.

Tony: A terrible thing, distrust.

Sidney: It certainly is.

> (*They push their plates to the two bruisers*)

Tony: Taste that.

(The bruisers taste a bit, then nod their OKs. Tony and Sidney eat)

Tony: I mean, if you can't trust each other, life's not worth living is it?

Sidney: No, it certainly isn't.

(They hand their cups of coffee to the bruisers, who sip them, savour them, and nod their OKs. Tony and Sidney drink)

Tony: Cheers.

Sidney: Good health.

Tony: I mean, friendship is based on trust, isn't it?

(They both reach for the butter dish — hesitate — and pass it to the bruisers, who stick their fingers in it to taste. They nod their OKs)

Sidney: Of course it is. What was it Byron said. . .?

(They pass the marmalade to the bruisers, who smell it and taste it, then hand it back)

Twelve Angry Men

First transmitted on 16 October 1959

Twelve Angry Men **featured**
SIDNEY JAMES
with
AUSTIN TREVOR
WILLIAM KENDALL
LESLIE PERRINS
PHILIP RAY
LEONARD SACHS
ROBERT DORNING
RALPH NOSSEK
ALEC BREGONZI
HUGH LLOYD
LALA LLOYD
MARIO FABRIZI
KENNETH KOVE
JAMES BULLOCH
BETTY CARDNO
MARIE LIGHTFOOT

Produced by DUNCAN WOOD

SCENE 1 An Old Bailey courtroom as seen in the television programme *The Verdict Is Yours*. The Judge is in full wig, there are ushers, clerks, Counsel's assistants, etc. A full High Court trial is in progress. The jury consists of three women (one neurotic, one an old lady), a military-looking gentleman, a company director, a farmer, a bank clerk, three other men (one old, another young) . . . and Sidney and Tony. Tony is the foreman of the jury. They are listening with great interest as the Prosecuting Counsel cross-examines an inspector of police in the witness box.

Prosecuting Counsel: Inspector Jones, will you tell the court in your own words the events leading up to the apprehension of the prisoner, John Harrison Peabody.

Inspector: Certainly. I was on patrol car duty on the night of the twenty-seventh when we received a radio message that the offices of the Hathaway Jewellery Company had been burgled. We immediately drove to their premises in Brook Street, and as we pulled up outside the store, the prisoner leapt from the doorway carrying numerous items of jewellery — exhibits one to thirty-seven, melud. We chased after the prisoner and tackled him and after a brief struggle he was taken into custody and charged with the felony.

Prosecuting Counsel: Thank you very much. No more questions. Your witness.

(*In the jury-box Tony gives Sidney an apple, and starts munching a sandwich*)

Tony: It's very well done, isn't it, just like *The Verdict is Yours*.

(*The Defending Counsel rises*)

Defending Counsel: The prisoner made a statement on arriving at the police station, did he not?

Inspector: He did.

Defending Counsel: What did he say in that statement?

Inspector: (*referring to a notebook*): He said, 'You've got the wrong man, guv. I was passing the shop when the burglar alarm went off and this geezer came running out and dropped the stuff. I picked it up and was just going to take it round the police station when you lot arrived.'

Defending Counsel: You were in plain clothes at the time, were you not?

Inspector: We were.

Defending Counsel: And what reason did the prisoner give for running away from you when you arrived?

Inspector: He said he thought we were Teddy boys.

(*The court laughs. Tony and Sidney roar with laughter*)

Tony: Oh dear, oh dear — (*turns to the rest of the jury*) — hear that? He thought they were Teddy boys. That's one in the eye for them. Oh, my goodness me. Dear oh dear.

(*The Judge raps with his gavel*)

Judge: Silence in court! I'm surprised at the foreman of the jury setting such a bad example. I thought at least he would show a little decorum.

Tony: (*rises*) Oh, I beg your pardon, your honour, I just thought it was rather amusing. I couldn't help it, it just slipped out. I mean, you had a little giggle yourself. . .

Judge: I did not have a little giggle.

Tony: You did, I saw you . . . you brought the end of your wig round to cover your mouth.

Judge: Please be quiet. This is a very serious case, it will shortly be your duty to judge this man. Please show the necessary intelligence and restraint required by the responsibility bestowed upon you.

(*Tony sits down, rather abashed*)

Sidney: You're not going to take that, are you? You're the foreman of the jury, he shouldn't make you look a Charlie in front of everybody. Go on, tell him.

(*Tony rises*)

Tony: Melud, I would remind you I am the foreman of this jury and as such you shouldn't make me look a Charlie in front of everybody.

Judge: Mr Foreman, I would remind you I am the Judge in this courtroom and as such I can replace you with somebody I regard as more competent.

(*Tony sits down*)

Sidney: Tell him he can't talk to you like that.

(*Tony rises*)

Tony: My friend says you can't talk to me like that.

Judge: I'm not the slightest bit interested in what your friend says. I am fully aware of my powers in this court, I know exactly what I can and what I can't do. I have been a judge now for over twenty years, and furthermore if you and your friend do not behave yourselves in a manner befitting members of the jury I will have you both thrown out of this courtroom and charged with contempt.

(*Tony sits down*)

Sidney: Tell him you'd like to see him try.

(*Tony rises*)

Tony: I'd like to . . . (*To Sidney*) You tell him.

Judge: You were going to say something?

Tony: No, no, nothing at all.

Judge: May we continue?

Tony: By all means, you carry on, mate.

Judge: Thank you. (*To Counsel*) Please continue.

One of comedy's most successful teams: Alan Simpson, Tony Hancock and Ray Galton in 1957   *Radio Times*

Hancock made the front cover of the *Radio Times* early in 1958 –
in Gogol's comedy, *The Government Inspector*, for Television World
Theatre on Sunday 9 February   *Radio Times*

Above: Kissing the bride – of BBC producer Dennis Main Wilson, on 1 October 1955   Dennis Main Wilson

Below left: With his first wife Cicely, at Heathrow Airport in 1961, just before Hancock flew to New York for the première of his film *The Rebel*.
Below right: Hancock was ten minutes late for his second wedding at the Marylebone Register Office on 2 December 1965; his patient fiancée was Freddie Ross   *Keystone Press Agency* and *Fox Photos*

Enjoying a joke during a break in rehearsal with Hattie Jacques and Sid James.
Hancock had just returned from a week's rest in a nursing home

Keystone Press Agency

Hancock photographed in 1960, when he was at the peak of his popularity.

Keystone Press Agency

Defending Counsel: Thank you. Exhibit No.1, please. These are the items of jewellery found on the prisoner's person?
  (*The usher takes the tray and shows them to the inspector*)
Inspector: Yes, they're the same ones.
Defending Counsel: Thank you. Perhaps the jury would like to see them.
Judge: The jury have already seen them once. As we are pressed for time, I don't think there is any need for them to see them again.
Sidney: (*to Tony*) How do we know they're the same ones we saw before? Tell him we *want* to see them again.
  (*Tony rises*)
Tony: How do we know they're the same ones we saw before? We want to see them again.
Judge: I assure you they are the same ones you saw earlier.
Tony: (*to Sidney*) He says they're the same ones.
Sidney: Tell him that's for us to decide. We're the jury.
Tony: That's for us to decide. We're the jury.
Sidney: Ask him if he wants a fair trial or not.
Tony: Do you want a fair trial or not?
Judge: This is a fair trial. The prisoner has not complained.
Tony: With all due respect, melud, nobody's asked the poor blighter. (*To prisoner, giving him the thumbs-up*) Don't you worry, mate, we'll see you get a fair trial. There'll be no withholding of evidence while I'm foreman.
Judge: We are not withholding evidence.
Tony: Then let us have another look at the exhibits. (*To jury*) Hands up who wants another butcher's at the evidence.
  (*The jury put their hands up*)
Tony: There you are, you've been out-voted. If this had been an election you would have lost your deposit there.
Judge: Oh, very well, show the exhibits to the jury. (*Leans over to usher*). Tell my wife I'll be a little late tonight.
  (*The usher takes the tray of jewellery over to Tony. He pokes over them, picks out a ring, and puts it on his finger to examine it. He shows it to Sidney who looks at it through a jeweller's eye-glass*)
Judge: (*exasperated*) Have you finished? Time is pressing and the rest of the jury have to examine it. Please put it back on the tray.
Tony: Yes, of course. (*He tries to get the ring off his finger but it is stuck. He struggles with it, to no avail. He laughs embarrassedly, but he still can't get it off*)
Judge: (*at the end of his tether*) Now what's wrong?
Tony: It's stuck, your honour, I can't get it off.
Judge: Oh, no! Why can't I have ordinary juries that do what I tell them, like other judges? Why does it always have to be me? Pull it, man.
Tony: I am pulling it. It won't budge. Have you got a bar of soap up there?
Judge: No, I haven't.
Tony: What about in your little room at the back? You must have a little bit in there. You must try and look a little lovelier each day, surely.
Judge: I haven't got any soap. You had no right to put the ring on your finger.
Sidney: Tell him there's no need to adopt that tone of voice.

Tony: You shut up. You've got me into enough trouble as it is. It's no good, it won't come off.

Judge: Oh, what a farce. Very well, show it to the rest of the jury, then try and get it off your finger. Continue, Mr Pritchard.

Defending Counsel: Thank you, my lord. I shall proceed with my final address to the jury.

Judge: Very well.

Defending Counsel: My lord, ladies and gentlemen of the jury, in all criminal procedures, it is the law of this land that to obtain a conviction the prosecution must prove beyond any reasonable shadow of doubt that the prisoner is guilty as charged . . . and this I respectfully submit they have failed to do. You must not . . .

(*He stops. Throughout his speech Tony and Sidney have been struggling to get the ring off Tony's finger. They are bending down behind the front of the jury box, talking in stage whispers. Tony is giving instructions on how to get it off. They realise they are being watched, and slowly emerge, embarrassedly*)

Judge: Have you finished?

Tony: I'm trying to get the ring off.

Judge: The Defending Counsel is talking to you.

Tony: Yes, but you told me to get the ring off. You can't have it both ways — either I get it off or I listen to him — what's it going to be?

Judge: You must listen to the Counsel. Get the ring off afterwards.

Tony: Right, well, as long as I know where I stand. Would you mind starting again?

Defending Counsel: (*to Judge*) Oh, really, do I have to?

Judge: I'm afraid so.

Defending Counsel: I was saying that the prosecution have not proved my client's guilt, and if there is any doubt at all about it, you are obliged under law to find him not guilty.

Tony: I've got you. Well, that's fair enough. I'll go along with that. May I ask a question, your honour?

Judge: Yes, what is it?

Tony: Have you got a bit of butter? I could have this off in a. . .

Judge: Be quiet and sit still! You are making a mockery of this courtroom. How you were ever elected foreman I shall never know.

Sidney: That's not very nice, is it? Ask him how he got made a judge.

Tony: No, I don't think I'd better.

Judge: Carry on, Mr Pritchard. And no more interruptions.

Defending Counsel: Thank you, melud. And so, members of the jury, I submit that the evidence the prosecution have put before you . . . (*Tony listens intently. The Defending Counsel addresses himself directly to Tony*) . . . is in no way conclusive of guilt, and I further submit that no jury can be asked to convict on such flimsy grounds. And in the light of this fact, I suggest that you can have no other alternative but to find my client not guilty and that he be discharged from this court a free man, without a stain on his character. I thank you.

(*Round of applause from Sidney and Tony*)

Tony: Very good, an excellent speech, my man, you should go far. A very engaging personality you have.

Defending Counsel: Thank you very much.

Tony: Right . . . next?

Judge: May I be permitted to decide on the procedure in this court? (*Sarcastically*) Or perhaps you would like to borrow my wig and take over?

Tony: (*rising*) Well, certainly, I don't mind taking a turn. I. . .

Judge: (*barks*) Sit down! Mr Spooner, would you care to sum up for the prosecution.

Prosecuting Counsel: Certainly, melud.

Tony: (*to Sidney*) I don't like this one. Dead smarmy, look at him. (*Mimics him*) 'Certainly, melud, oh, swipe me' — a crawler.

Prosecuting Counsel: I was very impressed by my learned friend's appeal for this man's innocence.

Tony: (*mimics him, to himself*) Oh . . . 'I was very impressed by my learned friend's appeal' — I'd like to put my foot right under his wig.

Prosecuting Counsel: It was very moving, eloquent, sentimental, maudlin, *rubbish*.

Tony: (*up on his feet*) I object!

Judge: It is not up to you to object or not object. Mind your own business. (*Tony sits down*) Continue, Mr Spooner.

Prosecuting Counsel: Thank you. The facts are quite plain — this man was caught red-handed outside the shop with the proceeds on him, he also has a long record for this kind of offence, he was also identified by the nightwatchman. It's an open and shut case and I therefore submit you have no alternative but to find him guilty as charged and put this vicious criminal beyond the reach of decent society. (*He sits down*)

Judge: Members of the jury, you have heard the evidence in this case. I would remind you that you are the sole judges of the fact. If there is any doubt in your minds whatsoever of this man's guilt, you must find him not guilty. If, however, you are satisfied that the prosecution have proved that he is guilty, then it is your duty to return such a verdict. I will now ask you to retire and consider your verdict.

Tony: May I ask a question, melud?

Judge: (*wearily*) What is it?

Tony: How long have we got?

Judge: I don't understand you.

Tony: I've seen this done on television. We go out, then, when the adverts are finished, we come back and tell you the verdict. So how long have we got?

Judge: You've got as long as you want.

Tony: That can't be right — they only get two minutes on television.

Judge: I don't care how long they get on television. This is not the same thing.

Tony: They said their programme was authentic. (*To jury*) Who can you believe, I ask you?

Judge: Will you please go and consider your verdict. Usher, please.

Usher: (*holds the book*) I will take this jury to some private and convenient place and shall not suffer anyone to speak to them, neither shall you speak to them yourself unless it be to ask them if they be agreed upon their verdict.

(*The jury files out through a door. Just before Tony disappears he turns back to the Judge*)

Tony: Would you send in a bar of soap? (*Points to his finger*) Some haircream, perhaps. I don't use it myself, perhaps you could help out . . . (*He goes out*)
(*The Judge wipes his forehead, completely exhausted*)

SCENE 2   The jury room. The twelve are seated round a long desk, Tony at the head, Sidney on his right. They have notepads and papers in front of them.

Tony: Right, ladies and gentlemen, we all heard what the Judge said — there's no need to hurry, we can take as long as we like, we won't be disturbed, our time is our own.

Sidney: (*brings out a pack of cards*). Good — what about a game of cards?

Tony: (*slaps his hand*) Put those away. We are here to decide whether that poor wretch out there is innocent or guilty.

Sidney: Well, let's cut for it, and get off home. Under a seven — he's guilty.

Tony: Under a seven he's — what sort of justice is that? What's the point of all that out there, all the lawyers with the wigs on and things, if all you've got to do is cut a seven and under? This is the Old Bailey, mate, not the Dodge House.

Military Gentleman: Well, come along, let's hurry it up, we don't want to be here all day.

Tony: Now, just a moment. We musn't be too hasty. It is essential to the cause of justice that we deliberate slowly and carefully before coming to any decision. Agreed?

Military Gentleman: Agreed.

Tony: Right.

Military Gentleman: Guilty.

Tony: Well, that wasn't much of a deliberation, was it?

Military Gentleman: As far as I'm concerned it's an open and shut case. The man is obviously guilty.

Tony: I think he's innocent. What do the rest of you think?

(One by one round the table they all say 'Guilty'. Sidney's turn comes)

Sidney: Guilty.

Tony: Et tu, Brute?

Sidney: Well, let's face it, they all say guilty. We'll be here for days if we disagree. Guilty. Let's get out of here, the pubs are open. We'll have time for a couple of pints down the Wig and Gavel.

Tony: That's not the right attitude. We are here to ensure that justice is done. That's what we're being paid for.

Sidney: Paid? Are we getting paid?

Tony: Of course we are. Thirty shillings a day.

Sidney: Thirty bob a day? Seven and a half nicker a week? Blimey, that's more that I get outside. Oh well, in that case, not guilty. Let's keep it going for as long as we can. We might be able to see the winter out.

Tony: I can't say I agree with your motives, but I agree with your decision. Any advance on two not guilties?

Company Director: Oh, this is ridiculous. Thirty shillings a day . . . it may be more than you earn, sir, but I am a company director, I am losing a fortune while this goes on.

Sidney: How can you put your personal gain above your duty as a citizen, you unfeeling swine? Doesn't justice mean anything to you?

Company Director: Of course it does, but the case against him is watertight. I don't see there's anything to discuss.

Sidney: Of course there is, there's loads to discuss. I reckon we've got seven or eight days of non-stop chat in front of us.

Bank Clerk: Oh, really, this is too much, he must be guilty.

Sidney: And I say he's not guilty.

Young Man: Of course he is.

Sidney: He isn't.

Company Director: He is.

Sidney: Do you want a punch up the bracket?

Company Director: How dare you!

(*A row breaks out*)

Tony: Please, please, Sid, you'll have the wallopers in here in a minute. A bounce-up in the Old Bailey — whatever next? You must control yourselves, I'm the foreman.

Military Gentleman: But he's talking a lot of nonsense, he wants to keep us here all week. The man is guilty, I demand. . .

(*Tony puts his finger up warningly*)

Tony: Ah, ah, ah! Who's the foreman?

Military Gentleman: (*grumpily*) You are.

Tony: That's it, then.

Military Gentleman: Yes, but I can't just sit here and let him. . .

Tony: Ah, ah, ah!

Military Gentleman: Yes, but I —

Tony: Ah, ah!

Military Gentleman: But —

Tony: Ah! We do not leave this jury room until we reach a unanimous decision from all of us. Now, the position is ten votes for guilty, two for not guilty. I think a discussion is called for to elaborate our points of view.

Company Director: Hear, hear.

Military Gentleman: Guilty.

Tony: I'll slosh you! I'm the foreman. I'll start. (*He rises*) We are gathered here today, to witness the joining together of . . . no, wrong opening. We are gathered here today to sit in judgment on a fellow human being. But before we have the temerity, nay, the audacity to take it upon ourselves to judge anyone, surely we must first judge ourselves. (*Looks around as if expecting a round of applause. Nothing. He carries on*) Are we, any one of us, so pure, so without sin in our own lives, that we are able to dispassionately, nay, objectively, nay — er — er — um — dispassionately judge another? I submit, therefore. . .

Company Director: Get on with it!

Tony: Do you mind? I was working up to a crescendo there. You mustn't interrupt people when they're approaching a crescendo. It can be very nasty, it could wreak havoc on one. Don't ever do that again. Where was I?

Sidney: You were submitting.

Tony: Oh, yes. I submit, therefore, that . . . what was I submitting?

Sidney: I don't know.

Tony: There you are, you see, it's gone now. I've forgotten what I was submitting. I'm submitless, utterly submitless.

Company Director: Good, now perhaps you'll be quiet and let us have a go.

Tony: All right, but just you watch your crescendo — I'll have you.

Company Director: Ladies and gentlemen. . .

Tony: Get on with it. (*Laughs*) Aha, that had him. He thought I was going to wait a bit, he knows what it's like now. Carry on.

Company Director: Ladies and gentlemen . . . (*Pauses and looks at Tony. Tony smiles and indicates the field is all his*) I. . .

Tony: Get on with it.

Company Director: Oh, this is intolerable. Are you going to allow me to speak or not?

Tony: All right, then, yes. I shall extend to him the courtesy he didn't extend to me. That'll show you how much better brought up I am than he was, out of the two of us in comparison with each other. Carry on.

Company Director: All I was going to say was that the evidence points unequivocally. . .

Tony: Pardon?

Company Director: Unequivocally. . .

Tony: Oh . . . all right, then . . . just watch it. Carry on.

Company Director: . . . points unequivocally to his guilt. Ten of us say he is guilty. The will of the majority should prevail as in any democracy. You should reverse your verdict to guilty.

Tony: Oh, I see, so that's the way the the wind's blowing. Might is right. Very well, I shall make my point. I am not voting against my conscience just to tidy it all up. As Pope Alexander says on Free Speech, 'To speak his mind, is every freeman's right, in peace, war, on the council, or when he's tight.' We'll go right round the table. You, Madam — you with the hat on.

Woman: Yes?

Tony: What do you think?

Woman: (*neurotic*) Guilty. Guilty. GUILTY. Send him away, he's a menace — put him away for as long as the law allows — make an example of him — there's too much namby pamby treatment of these thugs — bring back the cat. That'd stop them. I'd do it myself, if none of you men have the courage. Put him away, he's guilty, GUILTY.

Tony: So much for the gentler sex. You, sir. . .

Elderly Gentleman: (*meekly*) Well, I — er — I don't really know . . . I'm not sure now.

Tony: That's not good enough. He could have been your son — your own flesh and blood — the little boy you used to bounce up and down on your knee. It could have been him they're trying to send to a dark prison cell for fifteen years . . . no sun to light up his morning . . . out on the moor, the damp mist swirling round his ball and chain, breaking up huge boulders into little stones, then cementing little stones into big boulders for somebody else to break up into little stones . . . his wife putting his baby to bed . . . 'Where's Daddy, Mummy? Is he coming home tonight?' 'Hush, child, eat your piece of stale bread, and don't drop any crumbs on the sacking that forms your bedclothes.' 'Mummy, is that a tear I see trickling down your pale cheek?' ''Tis nothing, child, drink your spoonful of watered-down milk and go to sleep.' 'But Mummy, I want my Daddy, where have they put my Daddy?'

Sidney: (*tearfully*) Not guilty. Not guilty.

Tony: We've already got you, shut up. (*He turns back to the elderly man, resumes baby's voice*) 'I want my Daddy, where have they taken him? Please bring my Daddy back to me.'

Elderly Gentleman: Not guilty.

Tony: Got him. (*Sits down*) Nine–three. Anybody else want to come over to our side?

Company Director: You won't get me. Guilty.

Military Gentleman: Hear, hear — guilty. You won't get me with those cheap tricks.

Young Man: Nor me. Guilty.

Woman: Send him to jail.

(*The other 'Guilties' agree*)

Tony: Well, we appear to have reached a stalemate.

Sidney: Good, what about a game of cards? We've got plenty of time, let's enjoy ourselves. Let's get some booze in, have a party, get some more birds in.

Tony: Oh, be quiet, you licentious fool.

Farmer: Look, I suggest we go back and tell them we can't agree on a verdict.

Sidney: Then what happens?

Farmer: We can all go home.

Sidney: No, I'm not having that. I don't want to go home, I'm quite happy here. (*To Tony*) Thirty bob a day — go home — is he kidding?

Farmer: I can't stop here for ever. I've got a farm to run. There's the crops to get in. . .

Tony: Charming. You're prepared to give this man fifteen years just so you can go out and get your spuds in! The equation of human kindness: fifteen years equals two ton of King Edwards.

Farmer: But the man is guilty, he deserves to go to prison.

Tony: I don't think he is guilty.

Military Gentleman: But good heavens, why, man, why? Why do you persist in saying he's innocent in the light of the overwhelming evidence against him? Caught red-handed — identified — why, why?

Tony: Well, he's got such a nice face.

(*They all sit back, hopelessly frustrated*)

Military Gentleman: The man's hopeless. We'll be here all night.

(*Sidney picks up the phone*)

Sidney: Usher, send in twelve dinners.

Tony: Ask him if they've got a bit of lard. (*He points to the ring on his finger. Gives it a little tug*)

SCENE 3

The jury room, seven hours later. Sidney is playing patience. Tony is trying to get the ring off. The other ten are in various attitudes — some pacing up and down smoking, others sitting wearily round the table. The men have taken their coats off and loosened their ties. Their hair looks ruffled. All are looking tired out. The ash trays on the table are packed with cigarette ends.

Military Gentleman: Oh, good grief, man, how could it have been his twin brother ?

Tony: Well, it's a thought. It's happened before. It's like the Corsican brothers. One was good, and one was bad. I say we've got the good one.

Company Director: But he hasn't even got a brother.

Tony: That doesn't matter, we've all got doubles. There's a bookies' runner down our way, looks just like you.

Company Director: Thank you very much.

Tony: It's not you, is it?

Company Director: No, it's not.

Tony: Well, there you are, then.

Young Man: Oh, this is ridiculous. We're getting absolutely nowhere. We've been locked in this confounded room for seven hours now — seven hours. And what theories have you concocted? Twin brothers — doubles — black-outs — he was drugged by a gang of international crooks — he's the rightful heir to a European throne and they want him out of the way so they can put his uncle on —

Tony: Well, it's possible. His father used to sell onions. You don't know his family history. Who knows what his father did when he got off his bike in Boulogne? Straight up to a big chateau, on with the crown, up with the flag — Grand Duke of Burgundy. You never know.

Company Director: What do you mean, the Duke of Burgundy — they all live in Brixton.

Tony: They could have been exiled.

Military Gentleman: I give up. I give up. I don't want to speak to him any more. Just keep him out of my sight.

(*He turns his chair round and faces the other way in a sulk*)

Sidney: Well, that's eight–three and one retired hurt. (*Laughs*)

Farmer: Oh, this room is getting me down. I'm used to the open air, I'm suffocating in here.

(*Pause during which the farmer wanders over to the window. Tony gets up and follows him and Sidney goes and sits next to the young man*)

Tony: (*to farmer, looking out of window*) Lovely, isn't it, midnight over London?

Farmer: I'd sooner see it over my farm. How much longer do you think we'll be?

Tony: Who can tell? At this rate it could take weeks.

Farmer: Weeks? But I've got to be back on my farm tomorrow.

Tony: Well, there you are. Deadlock, isn't it? Nine–three.

(*Sidney and the young man are playing cards*)

Sidney: Your lead.

Young Man: How much longer do you think we'll be?

Sidney: Ooh, I don't know. Nine–three. Could take months. I heard of a case in Mexico . . . the jury were out for three years.

Young Man: Three years! It's impossible.

Sidney: No, straight up. It went through three revolutions and nine changes of government. One of the jury went bonkers with claustrophobia, three died of old age, and two of them were divorced by their wives for neglect. Are you married?

Young Man: Yes, I am.

Sidney: Oh dear. I hope she's patient. Three years is a long time. Your lead.

(Tony and the farmer are still looking out of the window)

Tony: Who's looking after the farm while you're away?

Farmer: My wife.

Tony: Country girl?

Farmer: No, she's a Londoner.

Tony: London! I don't suppose she knows much about farms, does she?

Farmer: No, she doesn't.

Tony: Yes. I bet it'll be looking a right mess when you get back. Dead chickens all over the place. Cattle lying on their backs with with their feet up. Tch, tch, tch.

Sidney: *(to young man).* How long have you been married, then?

Young Man: A week.

Sidney: Still, I wouldn't worry about it. If she loves you, she'll wait forever. After all *(savours it)* what's three years to a beautiful hot-blooded bride of twenty-one? That's a tanner you owe me. *(Pats him on the shoulder)* Good luck.

Tony: *(to farmer)* A Londoner, eh? Dear oh dear. I bet she's ploughed up the cornfields and put the pigs out to graze. Complete chaos, it'll be, financial disaster. Still, I admire you, you stick to your principles. You're a brave man. We could be out of here in ten minutes if everybody said not guilty. But you stick to your principles. Ruined but not dishonoured. Well . . . *(pats him on the shoulder)* Best of luck. *(He walks away, shaking his head, and making sure the farmer can hear him)* Poor devil.

(Sidney and Tony exchange thumbs-up signs. The farmer and the young man come up to Tony)

Farmer: I've changed my mind.

Young Man: So have I. There's not enough evidence. Not guilty.

Tony: Well done! Seven–five. Anybody else wavering?

Company Director: You won't get the rest of us so easily. We're equally determined as you are.

Tony: We shall see. We'll just sit it out.

(They settle back as if prepared for another long session. Tony starts singing 'For it's a long, long time from May till December')

★ ★ ★

SCENE 4

SCENE 4 The jury room. It is now four o'clock in the morning. The jurors are nearly asleep in their chairs. Nothing is happening. The clock is ticking audibly. Tony is tapping his pencil on the table. One of the 'Guilties' is twitching and ready to break. Suddenly he leaps up.

12th Man: I can't stand it any longer, it's driving me mad — this room — let me out — let me out — I want to go home. (*Rushes to the door, bangs on it*) Let me out . . . let me out . . .

(*The door is locked. He subsides hopelessly and totters back to the table. He sits down with his head in his hand. All through this Tony watches him, unconcerned. Then, when the drama has finished and the man is sitting down again. . .*)

Tony: Six all, I think.

Sidney: I think they're ready to break. Why don't you have another go?

Tony: Yes, good idea. (*Rises*) Ladies and gentlemen, the score is now six all. (*He adopts a barrister-like pose for his final address*) I will not go through the facts of this case again, save to suggest to you that there is some element of doubt as to this boy's guilt. As Shakespeare said in *The Merchant of Vienna* when Portion accused Shylock Holmes of pinching a pound of meat, 'The quality of mercy is not strained . . . it droppeth as the gentle rain from heaven . . .' (*points up*) 'upon the place beneath . . .' (*flutters his hand down to the ground*) 'it is twice blest, the sign of good . . . it is twice blest . . . it blesseth him that gives . . .'(*makes as though to give*) 'and him that takes' (*gesture of taking*). Take the Thomas who was sent to Coventry for looking through a keyhole at Lady Godiva. Can anybody prove he was looking at her? Can anybody prove it was he who shouted out, 'Get your hair cut'? Of course not. Sheer supposition. Does Magna Carta mean nothing to you? Did she die in vain; that gallant Hungarian peasant girl who forced King John to sign the pledge at Runnymede and closed all the boozers at half past ten? Is all this forgotten? No. My friends, it is not John Harrison Peabody who is on trial here today but the fair name of British justice. I ask you to send that poor boy back to the loving arms of his poor white-haired old mother . . . a free man. I thank you.

(*The jurors all applaud except for the military gentleman and the company director*)

Sidney: Hands up all those who say 'Not Guilty'.

(*They all put up their hands except for the same two*)

Tony: Ten–two, we're leading. It's just you two left.

Farmer: Yes, come on, who do you think you are? The man is innocent.

(*They all gather round shouting 'Innocent', 'Not Guilty', etc.*)

Company Director: Oh, very well, I can't stand any more of this. As much as I disagree with you all — all right. Let the criminal go free. I don't care. Let him loose so he can rob more shops — and houses. Your houses, perhaps. I don't mind.

Sidney: Not guilty, then?

Company Director: As you wish.

Sidney: Eleven-one. What about you? Oi — faceache.

Military Gentleman: Do what you like, I don't care.

Farmer: Well, there it is then — a unanimous verdict of not guilty. We can all go home.

(*They all cheer except Tony and Sidney. They notice Tony. They stop cheering*).

Young Man: What's the matter?

Tony: I've been thinking . . . about what he said (*points to company director*) . . . letting him go so he can rob other shops — and people's houses. I wouldn't like that on my conscience. I'm afraid I'll have to change my mind. Guilty.

Company Director: Oh, no, no, no! (*Holds head in hands*)

Sidney: Good boy. Eleven to one. We can all start again now.

Company Director: No, no, no — guilty. That's quite all right with me, we don't have to go through all that again, I'll go along with that — guilty. All in favour of guilty?

All: Yes!

Company Director: That's it, then. Everyone says guilty. It's all over.

Sidney: No, it's not. We're not packing up yet. Not guilty.

Company Director: He is guilty, we all agree he's guilty, your friend says he's guilty.

Sidney: I don't care. I'm counting on another five days' work out of this. Not guilty.

Company Director: (*nearly in tears*) Oh no! Not again. We can't go through all that again.

Sidney: I'll tell you what I'll do. If you'd all like to chip in thirty bob each to compensate my loss of earnings, I'll come in with you lot.

Company Director: (*eagerly*) Yes, all right, then. Certainly.

(*They feverishly rain thirty bob each in notes on Sidney. He collects it*)

Sidney: Gentlemen, we have just reached a unanimous verdict.

Tony: British justice has triumphed again. (*He goes round shaking hands*)

SCENE 5 The courtroom. The jury files back into the box.

Usher: The court will rise.

(*Everybody in court rises. The Judge comes through the door behind his bench, bows to the court and sits down. The court sits down*)

Judge: Carry on.

Usher: Who speaks as your foreman?

Tony: (*rises*) I am the foreman.

Usher: Have you agreed on a verdict?

Tony: We have.

Usher: Do you find the prisoner guilty or not guilty?

Tony: Guilty.

Usher: And that is the verdict of you all?

Tony: It is.

Judge: I will pass sentence after the recess. Court is adjourned. Er . . . just one moment. Mr Foreman, the ring, if you please.

Tony: Certainly . . . I've got . . . (*He feels on his finger for the ring. It's not there*) It's gone! It was on my finger. I shook hands with everybody . . . It was on my finger — I can't understand it. It must be somewhere . . . We were locked in for hours — it can't have flown away.

Judge: (*very stern*) Am I to take it the ring has disappeared? This is a very serious affair. The ring was exceedingly valuable. Is the police inspector in court?

SCENE 6 The courtroom. The Judge is at his bench. Before the court is a new trial. A new jury is in the box.

Judge: Carry on, Mr Farnsworth.

Usher: Put up the accused.

(*The door behind the dock opens and the previous jury files into the prisoner's dock one by one, led by Tony and Sidney. They crush themselves in tight*)

Usher: You have been accused of conspiring to steal a diamond ring valued at twenty thousand pounds. How do you plead?

(*Tony turns and mutters to them*)

Tony: I'm the foreman. Guilty. A prison sentence will be shorter than this trial.

Farmer: I want to get home to my pigs!

Young Man: What about my wife?

Tony: It wasn't my fault. Who's got the ring?

(*A fight breaks out amongst them all*)

The Big Night

First transmitted on 6 November 1959

The Big Night featured
SIDNEY JAMES
with
SAM KYDD
MICHAEL BALFOUR
PATRICIA HAYES
ROBERT DORNING
ANN LANCASTER
HUGH LLOYD
MARIO FABRIZI
ANNABELLE LEE
PADDY EDWARDS
IVOR RAYMONDE
JAMES BULLOCH
JOANNA DOUGLAS
TOM CLEGG

Produced by DUNCAN WOOD

SCENE 1
Tony's living-room, early morning. Sidney and Tony enter in dressing-gowns, full of joie de vivre, singing to themselves. Tony throws open the window and takes a deep breath.

Tony: Aaah, this is the life. Nine o'clock of a Saturday morning and all's well. (*Deep breath*) Ah . . . even the air smells different on a Saturday. (*Turns back to the room*) I love Saturdays. Best day of the week . . . no work . . . the weekend in front of you . . . and Saturday night to come. The big night. The one bright spot in a week of unrelieved misery. The one part of life's sordid panorama that I look forward to. A pound in your pocket, a pint in your hand, a bird on your arm, and the world is yours. By heavens, Sid, if it wasn't for Saturday night I'd go bonkers.

Sidney: Yeah, marvellous, isn't it. Oh, I can't wait to get into my pointed two-tones and off down the High Street. You feel like a king. A clean shirt on, new Peckham, a pair of luminous almond rocks, a new whistle, a nice crease in my strides, the barnet greased up, flashing the Hampstead Heath to all the bona palones. . .

IRELAND

Tony: I don't understand a word of what you're saying, but it sounds a sensation. Done up to the nines, wallowing in the myriad sensual delights that Cheam High Street has to offer a single lad of a Saturday night — the Las Vegas of South East England. You can't whack it. What's my girl like, Sid?

Sidney: I've already told you.

Tony: I know, but tell me again. I like to hear it. (*He closes his eyes as Sidney describes her*)

Sidney: Well, she's about five foot three or four . . . beautiful auburn hair (*Tony reacts blissfully throughout this description*) cascading down to her shoulders . . . Her face is like a Grecian goddess . . . Eyes like two limpid pools, challenging, inviting, smouldering . . . Her lips . . . the deepest red, soft, moist, clinging . . . A figure — that figure — when she walks it's like a young gazelle moving across the grasslands. Her voice — like a spring breeze, soft and gentle, murmuring . . . and her skin is the texture of a soft peach, vibrant, softer than the smoothest velvet. . .

Tony: What's her name?

Sidney: (*prosaically*) Gladys.

Tony: Oh, you always have to spoil it, don't you? Never mind, we'll be the toast of the coffee bars tonight. Toast — (*Yells out*) Oi! What about the breakfast, then?

(*Mrs Crevatte comes in carrying the breakfast. She slings it down in front of them*)

Mrs Crevatte: Here you are.

Tony: What's this mess supposed to represent?

Mrs Crevatte: That's oeufs scrambléd.

Tony: What sort of meal is this to put before two international playboys the like of us?

Mrs Crevatte: Take it or leave it, that's all there is.

Tony: Oh, really, this is Saturday, it's a special day . . . Why can't you give us something special for breakfast?

Mrs Crevatte: This is special . . . You wait till you see what you're getting on Monday.

Tony: Oh, very well. Go on, be off — we'll ring when we want you. (*Mrs Crevatte leaves*) Oeufs scrambléd! This isn't my idea of the grand life. I bet Noël Coward doesn't sit down to rubbish like this on a Saturday morning. He'd be sitting out on the balcony overlooking the Caribbean in his silk dressing-gown, sipping his iced orange juice through his long cigarette holder and tossing off nonchalant quips to a beautiful young lady. And what have I got? Oeufs scrambléd and Mrs Crevatte. There's no justice in this world.

Sidney: Never mind, we've still got tonight. And when you're sitting in the dark at the pictures on a Saturday night, you can be who you like.

Tony: Yes, it's funny how you always imagine you look like the bloke you've seen in the film, isn't it?

Sidney: Yeah . . . Remember last Monday — you came out convinced you looked like Robert Mitchum.

Tony: Oh, yes. . .

Sidney: You had your eyes half closed and nearly got run over, remember? Then on the Tuesday you saw *Gone With The Wind* — you opened your eyes, stuck your ears out, and started talking like Clark Gable.

Tony: Oh, yes, but fair do's. I do look a bit like Clark. Look, look — imagine the moustache . . . (*Holds his ears out with his forefingers*) See, see?

Sidney: Nothing like him.

Tony: Well, it's near enough. Who's on this week?

Sidney: Charlie Laughton.

Tony: Charlie Laughton? Do you know him personally, then? Charles Laughton to you. Yes, I've got him. (*Makes face like Charles Laughton*) 'Mr Christian . . . I'll have you swinging from the highest yard-arm in the British Navy.'

Sidney: Charles Laughton? It's no use looking like him down the Palais on a Saturday night — a bit of glamour, that's what you want. (*Gets up*) Gene Kelly . . . (*Sings*) 'I'm singing in the rain, just singing in the rain . . . ' (*Does a bit of soft shoe dancing*) Eh? Eh?

Tony: (*laughs*) Whoo, whoo — Gene Kelly — *him*? Har har har. Oh dear, the best laugh I've had in years. Let's face it, Sid, with a face like that, you couldn't look like anybody else except you. Play your best card — intriguing ugliness — that's the only chance you've got.

Sidney: You've got a sauce! I'm not ugly — there's quite a lot of women find me very attractive.

Tony: Yes, but only women who aren't as good-looking as you — and they're few and far between, poor devils.

Sidney: We'll see tonight. You watch me — I'll slay them. You watch the old James technique come into play. . .

Tony: Yes, you drug them, don't you?

Sidney: I do not! I charm them. I give them the chat. One night out with me and a shopgirl becomes a princess. A couple of choruses of 'Come Prima' down their earhole and they're mine, mate.

Tony: Well, I wish you the best of luck, Sid. If we play our cards right this should be the best Saturday night in years. All dressed up and raring to go. Oh, I am looking forward to it. We're going to crawl back here in the early hours of the morning with a smile of blissful contentment on our faces. (*He picks up a little tiny handbell and rings it delicately. Mrs Crevatte enters*) You may clear away and bring in the coffee.

Mrs Crevatte: You haven't touched it.

Tony: No, scrape it over the fence for next door's dog. I've never liked him.

Mrs Crevatte: Are you two going out tonight?

Tony: We are. We always go out on Saturdays. It's our big night. You may lay out my chalk-striped flare-line with the handstitched lapels. I shall be wearing that tonight.

Mrs Crevatte: You won't.

Tony: I beg your pardon?

Mrs Crevatte: I sent it to the cleaners.

Tony: Oh no! There was no need, it was perfectly spotless. Oh, very well, I shall wear my Prince of Wales demob suit.

Mrs Crevatte: That's at the cleaners as well.

Tony: What? My entire wardrobe at the cleaners? You'll just have to go down and get them.

Mrs Crevatte: I haven't got time, I'm off home in a minute. I've got my old man's breakfast to get.

Tony: But I'll have nothing to wear tonight. We're going out, I've got to have my suits.

Mrs Crevatte: I can't help it, I'm not going to get them.

Tony: Sid — you'll have to go and pick them up. The Dreadnought Dry Cleaners and Bagwash Ltd.

Mrs Crevatte: He can't go.

Tony: Why?

Mrs Crevatte: I took all his suits down there as well. He asked me to.

Sidney: Oh, cor blimey!

Tony: You didn't, Sid?

Sidney: Well, I thought when you went to pick yours up, you could collect mine as well. I didn't know she was taking all of yours.

Tony: So we haven't got a stitch to wear between us. How are we going to manage?

Sidney: We'll just have to go down and get them.

Tony: How? How can we walk down Cheam High Street in our dressing-gowns? Mrs Crevatte. . .

Mrs Crevatte: No, no, I'm off. I'm late as it is. (*Goes to the door*) I'll pick them up on Monday for you. Have a good time. Bye bye. (*She leaves*)

Tony: Have a good time? Doing the Blue Tango in your pyjamas? Ruined everything, she has.

Sidney: No, she hasn't. We'll go and get them ourselves — come on.

SCENE 2
The street. Tony and Sidney are walking fast as though in a road race. They are wearing white running shorts and singlets with numbers on their belts. They go into a dry cleaning shop.

SCENE 3
The living-room. Tony and Sidney enter in their running shorts, carrying cleaning boxes. They are breathless.

Tony: Beat you!

Sidney: No, you didn't. I was held up by the zebra crossing.

Tony: Well, I got stopped at the traffic lights. It was my tactics that beat you. I saved myself for the last burst.

Sidney: You were nearly running!

Tony: I was not. I brought my heel down every time. Beat you fair and square.

Sidney: Well, anyway, we got the suits. We'll be all right for tonight now. All cleaned up and pressed.

Tony: I know. Dapper we'll be, dead dapper. A vision of sartorial elegance. We'd better get the clean shirts out, give them an airing.

Sidney: Be careful with them, we don't want to get them dirty. There's nothing puts the little darlings off more than a grubby drip-dry.

Tony: Quite, quite. Still, I think we'd better get them out now in case we have a mad rush tonight. Get the links and stiffeners in while they're off, not while they're on. Have you ever tried to put a stiffener in once you've got your tie on? Very hard . . . you can strangle yourself. I remember once I had a bent stiffener and I tried to. . .

Sidney: Yeah, all right, some other time. Get the shirts out and stop nattering.

(Tony goes over to the airing cupboard, opens it, and a pile of dirty washing falls out. He picks up a shirt)

Tony: Stone me, she hasn't done the washing! Look at this lot — they should have been pinned up with a little bit of cardboard under the collar. She's a lazy so and so . . . I pay her to do the washing and she hasn't touched it. We can't go out in linen this colour.

Sidney: We'll have to wash them. . .

Tony: And how long is it going to take to dry? You can't wear damp shirts. We'll get rheumatism with this lot on our back — we'll seize up long before the band gets to 'Who's taking you home tonight?' Who's taking you home tonight — the St John's Ambulance, mate. We've had it . . . She's a fool, that woman, she'll have to go. . .

Sidney: Oh blimey, surely there must be some way we can get them washed, dried and pressed before tonight. Let's see now. . .

SCENE 4   **The launderette. All the machines are in use, with the owners of the washing sitting opposite their machine. Tony and Sidney enter self-consciously. They go up to the counter. There is a weighing machine.**

Woman: Good morning, sir.

Tony: Good morning. My friend and I wish to launder our soiled linen.

Woman: Certainly, sir. Nine pounds for two-and-nine. Would you put your washing on the weighing machine, please.

(*Tony puts his shirt on the machine*)

Tony: Four ounces. That'll be about a pennyworth. (*Puts his hand in his pocket*)

Woman: Two-and-ninepence is our minimum charge.

Sidney: Two-and-nine for one shirt? Cor blimey, that's more than he paid for it.

Tony: Do you mind? What I pay for my chemiserie is my own business. A little bit of Empire preference never hurt anybody. Two-and-three is quite enough to pay for a shirt. I'm not made of money. Now we're not going to get our extra ten shillings a week when we're sixty-five, some of us have got to watch our pennies. Can't you do it for less than two-and-nine?

Woman: I'm sorry, sir. But your friend could put his shirt in with yours, that would save you hiring two machines.

Sidney: I should coco! I'm not putting mine in with that cheap old bit of burlap.

Tony: How dare you! Best quality parachute panel, that is. And it's transparent. They go berserk when they see my string vest through this.

Woman: Well, that's two machines, two-and-nine-each.

Tony: Sheer extortion. (*They pay and go over to their machines. They start examining the machine from all angles. Finally Sidney manages to get his door open. Tony still struggles*) Oh, I can't keep up with modern science. How do you get inside?

Sidney: Come here . . . (*Sidney shows him*) You put your shirt in there.

Tony: Are you sure it's safe?

Sidney: Of course it is.

Tony: I'm entitled to ask. You always snap my head off, you do. (*They put their shirts in and close the door*) Now what do we do?

Sidney: Nothing, you just switch on and sit there.

Tony: What, no scrubbing or squeezing or anything like that?

Sidney: No, you just sit back and wait till it's done.

(*Tony switches on*)

Tony: Well, isn't that marvellous? When I think of my poor old mother on the side of the canal with two big stones, pounding away there, I boggle.

Sidney: Yes, well, that's progress for you.

Tony: Yes. Well, I won't need these, then, will I? (*He takes two great round smooth* *stones from his carrier bag)* I'll put them back in the path when we get home. (*They sit down*) Well, this is marvellous, isn't it? I'm going to enjoy this. I think I'll come down here every week. (*He settles back*) Ooooh, look — you can see it going round inside — look. Look, there it goes . . . that was the collar . . . there's the sleeve . . . it'll be round again in a minute. There it is — ha ha, oh dear! Can you see yours going round, Sid?

Sidney: (*uninterested*) Yeah, yeah.

Tony: Oh, I wish I'd known about these before. My goodness, this is money well spent, this is. (*Nudges the man next to him*) That's my shirt going round in there. Look, there it goes, see? They're very good, aren't they? Of course, they're very simple really. . . (*Very knowledgeable*) The basic principle of the thing is very elementary — it was very well known in the time of the Phoenicians — it's a spindle with a rotary arm — of course, they had a rope tied to a camel going round in a circle, but it's the same idea, the centrifugal force creating a disturbance in the water. . .

Sidney: Shut up.

Tony: I was just telling the gentleman about the camels, that was all. I wasn't doing any harm . . . (*To the man, in a confidential tone*) He's very touchy — he doesn't like me speaking to strangers.

1st Man: Neither do I.

Tony: Oh. Yes. (*He casts his eyes heavenwards, then settles back, and quiet reigns. Then he starts getting interested in the man's washing going round. He leans forward and studies it. The man watches him suspiciously. Tony catches the man's look and pretends he wasn't looking at his machine*)

1st Man: *That's* your machine.

Tony: Yes, yes, that's right, yes.

1st Man: What were you looking at mine for, then?

Tony: Well — er — I — nothing, I — It made a change, that's all. I got fed up with looking at my own.

1st Man: You don't want to be so nosy, do you? Looking at other people's washing, whatever next?

Tony: I wasn't really — I mean, you can't see, anyway — well, I was just bored, that's all. . .

1st man: Would you like me to stop the machine, take them out and hold them up for you?

Tony: No, no, that's not necessary. There's no need to go to those lengths — I'm not really interested in your washing . . . You just seemed to be getting a better picture on yours. (*Laughs. The man just stares at him, stonily*) Oh, cor.

(*An attendant comes up*)

Attendant: Is there anything wrong?

1st Man: Yes, it's him. He's looking at my washing.

Tony: No, I wasn't . . . I'm not in the least bit interested in his ablutive activities. I was merely trying to ascertain if he puts his coloureds in with his whites. It's the first time I've been in one of these establishments. And another thing. He's got more water than I have. That's not right for a start.

1st Man: I've got more washing in there, it makes it look as if I've got more water. It's the displacement.

Tony: We won't go into Archimedes' Principle. What about all those bubbles? I haven't got any bubbles. Sid, have you got any bubbles?

Sidney: Yeah, hundreds of them.

Tony: Well, I haven't got any bubbles. (*To a woman further up*) Have you got any bubbles, dear? (*She sniffs and ignores him*) Why haven't I got any bubbles?

Attendant: Did you put enough soap powder in?

Tony: Soap powder? What soap powder?

Attendant: I gave your friend two portions of soap powder.

Tony: (*to Sidney*) How dare you filch my soap powder! That's not very nice, is it? Pinching a chap's soap powder. You're trying to make me look tatty tonight, you're trying to make your shirt look whiter than mine, so when you stand next to me people'll start singing about my mother. Well, I'm not having that — give me a ladleful of your bubbles. (*He picks up a ladle, goes over to Sidney's machine, lifts the lid and sticks the ladle in. He scoops out a ladle of bubbles. Sidney grabs him*)

Sidney: Put those bubbles back!

Tony: Half of them are mine.

Sidney: Put them back.

Tony: No. (*He quickly empties the bubbles into his machine*) There.

Sidney: (*closing the lid of his machine*) You're not getting any more. (*He sits on the top of his machine*)

Tony: I haven't had my full whack. (*He tries to pull Sidney off the machine*)

Attendant: Please, please, you're creating a disturbance. I'm responsible for these machines, you'll damage them. Here you are . . . you can have some soap powder. (*He puts some soap powder in Tony's machine*)

Tony: Oh . . . thank you very much. I'm sorry I caused a scene. It's just that I have very strong feelings on questions like this . . . a man is entitled to his fair share of bubbles. . .

Attendant: Quite, quite. I'm sure everything will be all right now. Why not sit down, and watch your shirt going round.

(*Tony sits down, mollified, and everything is back to normal again. The seat next to Tony is now vacant. A man walks in carrying a bag*)

2nd Man: Excuse me, old man, have you got much washing in your machine?

Tony: One shirt, that's all.

2nd Man: Oh good, I've got a shirt I want washed, it's not worth paying the full price . . . Would you mind very much if I slipped it in with yours?

Tony: Well, I don't know. . .

2nd Man: It won't make much difference, will it, two shirts instead of one?

Tony: All right then, yes, carry on, mine's nearly finished any way.

2nd Man: Thank you very much.

(*He takes off his coat, hangs it fastidiously over a chair. He opens Tony's machine, tips some powder into it, then takes off his shirt and pops it in the machine. He sits next to Tony in his singlet and starts reading a magazine. Tony watches all this with mute astonishment. He shrugs to Sidney*)

Tony: We've never had it so good?

Sidney: (*getting up*) Well, that's it, they'll be finished by now.

Tony: Well, that was quick, wasn't it? The camels used to take all day . . . mind you, I don't think they used to whip round as fast as this lot do. Well, well, a most instructive morning. How do we get it out?

Sidney: Same way as you put it in.

Tony: Oh yes. (*He stops the machine. Takes a shirt out. Holds it up*) Perfect. Perfect.

2nd Man: Excuse me, old man, that's my shirt.

(*Tony examines it*)

Tony: So it is. I do beg your pardon. (*He reaches in and pulls out his own shirt — piece by piece — one arm, then another arm, then the front panel, the back panel and the collar*) Look what's happened to my shirt!

Sidney: (*laughing*) What can you expect for two-and-threepence?

Tony: I'm not having this . . . I shall demand compensation. They can't destroy people's shirts willy-nilly. Where's the manager? (*A man walks up*)

Manager: Is anything wrong, sir?

Tony: There is indeed. Look at this. (*He holds up the remnants of his shirt*) Your machine has done this. I demand recompense.

Manager: What's the point in putting it in like that? It's a washing machine, not a sewing machine.

Tony: How dare you! The man's a fool. A brand new shirt, the first time it's been washed.

Manager: Then I suggest you buy better shirts in future.

Tony: Are you asking for a punch up the faghole, mush? Are you going to replace this shirt or not?

Manager: I'm sorry, sir, it is quite clearly stated on the outside, 'Customers use our machines at their own risk.' There is nothing I can do about it.

Tony: But this is the only clean shirt I've got . . . I'm going out on the town tonight, I can't go bird-watching in a thing like this.

Manager: Might I suggest you wear the front part, which is in fairly good condition, then do your jacket up like this. (*Pulls Tony's lapels together*) You won't notice all the shirt isn't there, and it does give the suit a rather Italian flavour.

Tony: Yes, but I'll be self-conscious, I'll know the truth. I wouldn't be comfortable in the knowledge. You can't go around doing the George Sanders with only half a shirt on.

Manager: That's all I can suggest, sir. Now, if you'll excuse me, I'm a very busy man . . . Oh, if you'd like to dry the pieces, the spin drier is over there for only a penny extra.

Tony: I'm not taking any chances with the rest of it. I want a shirt, not a bag of confetti. I should have stuck to the two big stones, at least you know where you are. Good day to you, sir. (*He stalks out*)

SCENE 5 Tony is kneeling by the bank of a stream with two big stones, pounding the life out of his shirt.

SCENE 6 Tony's living-room. He comes in holding the stones and carrying the shirt. He is wringing his finger which he has obviously smashed.

Sidney: How did you get on?

Tony: Oh, hopeless. Four buttons and a finger gone. You'll just have to go by yourself, Sid. I'd only spoil it for you . . . The girls won't look at you if your friend's walking around without a shirt on.

Sidney: I can't take two birds by myself . . . I can't afford it for one thing, and you can't do any good anyway. You can't do any courting with the other one standing there swinging her handbag, and whistling. You've got to come out, we won't get another chance till next Saturday. Look, you don't have to wear a shirt. You could wear your jersey . . . and a muffler. . .

Tony: Charming. And a bit of pie done up in a spotted handkerchief slung over my shoulder, and what about the front of my boot opened up with the nails poking out . . . and a top hat with the lid sticking up?

Sidney: Well, I'm only trying to be helpful.

Tony: Well, don't . . . I've got to work this out myself. How can one get over not having a shirt to wear? I've got it! A polo-necked sweater, corduroy trousers and sandals . . . A beatnik, that should get them going. I bet they've never been out with a beatnik before.

Sidney: What's a beatnik do, then?

Tony: I don't know, but as long as they don't know either, they can't argue, can they? Right, then, that's settled. I'll go down the barbers and get a haircut and a shave and I'll meet you outside the pictures tonight.

Sidney: Haircut and shave? What for? Beatniks don't worry about things like that.

Tony: Ah well, I'm not a proper beatnik, I must have a haircut and shave . . . I'm more of a bourgeois beatnik. I'm confident again now . . . I've got a feeling they're going to be dead chuffed when they see me. Tell me again, what's mine like?

Sidney: I've told you . . . three times.

Tony: Oh yes . . . All right then, I'll see you down there. Oh, and Sid — try and do something with yourself, Sid, don't show me up.

(*Sidney's face registers his reaction to this*)

SCENE 7 Outside the cinema. Sidney is waiting there looking very smart in a good suit, natty tie. He is very pleased with himself. He straightens his tie, smooths back his hair, arranges his jacket. He looks at his watch. Tony comes up. He has a big false beard on. A shirt collar is sticking up over a crew-necked sweater.

Sidney: It's about time you turned up, you're ten minutes late, I've been . . . (*Notices the beard*) What's that for?

Tony: Leave it alone. I've got no choice. Look . . . (*He pulls down the beard. On his chin are three bits of sticking plaster*) That fool of a barber! He did it on purpose, I'm sure he did. Everything was all right until we got on to politics, and I finished up a mass of cigarette papers. (*He lets the beard go back*) And look at the hair. (*Shows Sidney the back of his head*) The thirty-nine steps.

Sidney: Well, you can't wear that. I told them what you looked like, and I didn't say anything about a beard. Take it off.

Tony: No, I can't go around with a faceful of sticking plaster. The beard's quite in keeping with the rest of the outfit. In fact, if it goes down well tonight, I shall grow one of my own.

Sidney: Look, take my word for it, you look a right twit. (*He lifts the false beard up and sees Tony's collar*) Here, I thought you didn't have a shirt? (*He pulls the collar. It comes off*)

Tony: You great oaf! I spent three-quarters of an hour getting that in place (*Wriggles*) Oh, this sweater is ridiculous without a shirt on, it's like a tribe of ants tramping all over you. (*Scratches himself. He pulls the sweater over his head and tries to fix the collar back into place. His head is covered completely by the sweater*)

(*Two girls come up*)

1st Girl: Hallo, Sid.

Sidney: Hallo, Gladys, how are you?

1st Girl: Sorry we're late. This is my friend, Elsie.

Sidney: Hallo, Elsie.

2nd Girl: Has your friend turned up yet?

(*Tony's head appears out of the top of his sweater as he pulls it down*)

Sidney: This is him.

Tony: How do you do?

(*The girls stare at him*)

2nd Girl: Yes . . . well, cheerio, then.

Sidney: Where are you going?

1st Girl: We've just remembered, we've got to be home early.

Sidney: Well, that's all right . . . what time?

2nd Girl: Now. Come on.

(*They leave in a hurry. Tony takes the beard off*)

Tony: So that was Gladys and Elsie . . . Oh well, it was pleasant while it lasted.

Sidney: Well, cor blimey, that's not very nice, is it? Standing us up like that.

Tony: I'm not surprised, it's always the same when I go out with you, you always put them off. Look at you — fancy wearing a tie like that, and those horrible shoes — what self-respecting young lady wants to be seen with a sight like you? I thought you would have learnt by now, why don't you do something with yourself, honestly . . . You spoil it for me. . .

Sidney: Well, of all the nerve! You turn up here looking like the second mate off a French tramp steamer and you have the sauce to complain about me. . .

Tony: Look, there's no point in pulling each other to pieces, we all know the truth. You just don't know how to dress, you never have done, and you've completely ruined our big night. We might just as well go home.

Sidney: Don't let's give up yet, the night is young . . . Let's go in the pictures, you never know, there might be some spare stuff inside floating around . . . and with the lights down, you won't be so much of a lumber. The best thing for you to do is to catch them when they first come through the curtains because they can't see a thing then. Just let them get a sniff of the after-shave lotion and we've got them.

Tony: All right then, one last try.

(They go into the foyer of the cinema and up to the pay box. The manager comes up to them)

Manager: Just a minute, where do you think you're going?

Sidney: Where do you think we're going . . . inside.

Manager: *You* might be . . . he's not.

Tony: I beg your pardon?

Manager: We don't allow scruffs inside our cinema. We've had quite enough trouble round these parts as it is. Come on out.

Tony: Take your hands off me.

Manager: I know your type — ripping the seats — tripping up the ice-cream girl — well, you're not doing it in here.

Tony: I am not a hooligan.

Manager: What are all those bits of plaster on your face?

Tony: They're razor scars.

Manager: Oh, you admit it. Trying to get away from a gang, no doubt . . . they'll all be in here looking for you. Oh no, this is a respectable cinema, we're not having the likes of you inside, dressed like that.

Tony: Oh, come now, do I look like a Teddy boy? I am a perfectly respectable law-abiding citizen. This mode of dress has been forced upon me by circumstances. . .

Sidney: Look, I'll take responsibility for him. I'll see he doesn't slash the seats up.

Manager: Well . . . all right, then. But no whistling or stamping your feet in the love scenes.

Tony: You're not convinced, are you?

Sidney: Oh, come on . . . *(Goes to the pay box, gets the tickets and they go inside)*

SCENE 8 Inside the cinema. The audience is scattered about, with plenty of empty seats. Tony and Sidney grope their way in.

Tony: Hold my hand, I can't see. Are there any steps here?

Sidney: No, no, you're all right. Don't go right down the front . . . Sit here, we can have a look round.

(There are two seats in the back row half way along. They move into the row, disturbing the other people)

Tony: Excuse me, thank you very much.

(Two people start coming in from the other gangway. They see Tony and Sidney

making their way along and the four of them hurry up to get to the two seats first. The other two make it, and Tony and Sidney are left standing in the row. A man who is sitting where they are standing pokes his head round them)

Man: Are you going to stand there all night?

Tony: Oh dear — thank you — excuse me. . .

(Tony and Sidney make their way back to the gangway)

Sidney: Here you are . . . we'll sit here. . .

(There are two seats on the gangway in the next row down. Tony and Sidney sit in them. Immediately they start looking round the cinema to see who's there. Sidney suddenly spots two girls sitting on their own a couple of rows further down)

Sidney: Look, down there . . . two little darlings on their own.

Tony: Where, where, where?

Sidney: Four rows down.

Tony: Oh yes, I see them.

Sidney: I don't think much of yours. Still, come on. . .

(They get up and go down the gangway to the row the two girls are in. They move along the row. Sidney sits down on one side of the girls and Tony on the other. No sooner have they sat down. . .)

Girl: This is where we came in, Ethel. Come on. Excuse me. . .

(They get up and push past Tony and go out. Sidney and Tony are now left with two seats between them)

Tony: It's just not our night, is it? *(They start looking round again)* Do you think it's best to split up, or hunt in a pack?

Sidney: I think it'd be best to split up.

Tony: All right, but if you find anything, hoot like an owl, you know . . . (*Hoots like an owl*)

Member of audience Ssshh . . . be quiet!

Tony: Oh, go home. (*To Sidney*) Well . . . good hunting. (*They shake hands dramatically. Then they split up and go their separate ways*)

SCENE 9 Outside the cinema. Tony and Sidney are slung out of two different exits by two commissionaires.

Tony: I'll have the law on you — you can't manhandle people like that! How was I to know it was the manager's wife?

Commissionaire: Get out and don't come back.

Sidney: Well, you don't expect us to sit still and watch that rubbish you're showing.

Tony: Don't expect me to patronize you any more. Not a penny, sir. I shall go elsewhere for my drinks on a stick. Come, Sidney, don't let us stand here chit-chatting with these uniformed yobs.

(*The commissionaires go back inside the cinema*)

Sidney: Well, what do we do now?

Tony: Let's draw a moustache on Susan Hayward and run for it.

Sidney: What a miserable night out this has been. To think I've been looking forward all week to this.

Tony: Oh, stop moaning, it's the same for me. (*Looks at poster*) *I Want to Live.* Stone me, do you call this living? Saturday's nearly finished. And there isn't another one for seven days.

Sidney: There's still time to find a couple of girls.

Tony: Of course there isn't. Ten o'clock — all the spare stuff will be fixed up by now. Believe me, I know from experience, if there's anything left after ten o'clock, it's rubbish. Let's face it, Sid, our big night has been a complete and utter fiasco. Let's go home, go to bed, and forget all about it.

(*Two policewomen in uniform walk past and have a look at the stills. They are good-looking girls*)

Sidney: They're all right, aren't they?

Tony: Yes, very nice.

Sidney: What do you reckon, then?

Tony: Wouldn't stand a chance — how could we get off with them? They'd run us in.

Sidney: What better way of getting acquainted? It's a lovely long walk to the station.

Tony: Oh no, Sid — it's not worth it. Let's go home.

Sidney: No, faint heart never won fair lady. It'll only cost us a couple of nicker fine. . .

Tony: What will?

(*Sidney picks up a brick*)

Sidney: This. . .

Tony: No, Sid, no!

(*Sidney throws the brick through a window in the cinema*)

Sidney: Here we are, over here. . .

(*They hold out their hands towards the policewomen. Two policemen come in from the opposite direction and grab them*)

Policeman: All right, come on, you two — another couple of drunks — come on, down the station.

Tony: Just a minute — we're being arrested by those two — we're booked. That's the only reason we did it.

Policeman: Are you coming quietly? There's too much hooliganism going on round here.

Tony: But we want to be arrested by those two young ladies over there.

Policeman: Yes? Well, that's my missus.

Tony: I should have known. Stone me, what a fiasco. The Big Night! (*An idea hits him – he knocks the policeman's helmet off*)

Policeman: Here, here, what's all that about?

Tony: Never you mind. Well, that should take care of next Saturday as well. I'm not having this again. (*To policeman*) Come on, then, what are we hanging about for?

(*They walk off*)

The Cold

First transmitted on 4 March 1960

The Cold featured
SIDNEY JAMES
with
JOHN LE MESURIER
PATRICIA HAYES
HUGH LLOYD
ANNE MARRYOTT
TOM CLEGG
HERBERT NELSON

Produced by DUNCAN WOOD

IRELAND

SCENE 1

Tony's living-room. Tony is sitting at the table with his head covered by a cloth and stuck into a bowl. There is steam rising from the bowl. He emerges from the bowl, coughs and splutters a few times. He is worn out from a streaming cold. He groans weakly and dives back into the bowl. After a few seconds he emerges again. He is wrapped in an overcoat with a tartan blanket draped round his shoulders. He coughs again.

Tony: Oh cor . . . dear oh dear! Stone me . . . this is hopeless.

(*He takes a spoonful of mixture from a bottle. He looks at his watch. On the table he has a vast collection of various pills, mixtures, etc. He takes pills from several boxes, then takes a swig of various mixtures. He sniffs from a Benzedrex inhaler. He mixes up a powder and drinks it, coughs a bit more, and plunges back under the cloth into the bowl. Sidney enters*)

Sidney: What's the matter with you?

Tony: I don't know, I think I've got a cold coming.
> (*Takes a few more pills. Starts coughing again*)
Sidney: Oh, cor blimey, do you have to make so much noise?
Tony: (*angry*) I can't help it. I'm ill. Do you think I enjoy sitting here coughing
my ribs up? Haven't you got any sympathy for the afflicted?
Sidney: Sympathy? So you've got a cold. What's a cold? Everybody gets colds.
Tony: Not like I get them.
Sidney: Of course they do.
Tony: They do not. Samples, that's all they get. Me, I get the full output of the
entire germ kingdom. Millions of them, all the big indestructible ones, flags
waving, on the march, straight up my hooter. A complete conquest, it is. All
my resistance goes. Scattered to the remote parts of my body. All me red
corpuscles hiding behind corners, frightened to come out. And I don't blame
them, up against the sort of germs I get — those ones with hairy legs and pointed
teeth like in those kitchen sink adverts.
Sidney: I don't suppose all that old rubbish you keep taking helps you any.
Tony: What, these? These are all tried and tested. These are the only things
between me and the black Rolls-Royce, mate.

Sidney: Dah, that's all a load of old rubbish. None of that stuff there can kill cold germs.

Tony: No, but it might wake my lads up a bit, get them regrouped for a counter-attack. Now, if you'll excuse me, it's about time I submerged again. Whoop, whoop, whoop, whoop, whoop. (*He dives into the bowl with the cloth over his head. Suddenly he emerges from the bowl in a right state, nearly choking*) My back. . . (*Indicates his back*) Hit it. . . (*Coughs*)

(*Sidney is worried and jumps across and bashes his back, pounding the life out of Tony*)

Tony: (*recovering*) Oh dear . . . I think I stayed under too long. I'll have to take a snorkel down next time. Oh, that was a nasty moment. The fumes got me.

Sidney: Serves you right. Why don't you throw all this stuff out of the window? It's doing you more harm than good. Look at it. (*Picks up a bottle*) Koffitup Kold Kapsules. With a 'K'. 'Take twenty tablets every half an hour, an extra twenty before meals, and a boxful before going to bed. Warning, it is dangerous to exceed the stated dose.'

Tony: (*looks at his watch*) Ooh, it's a good job you reminded me. Count out a couple of hundred, will you, I'm a few hours behind.

Sidney: You're not to take any more. You'll sound like a pair of maracas.

Tony: They're doing me good. They clear the bloodstream and lubricate the bronchial tubes so as to prepare the way for half a glass of this. (*Hands him a bottle*)

Sidney: (*reads*) 'Dr Harvey McConnell's Lung Syrup'. That sounds like a lot of old jollop.

Tony: Old jollop? World famous, that is. My old grandmother used to swear by Dr McConnell's Lung Syrup. She drank a bottle a day for the whole of her life. She couldn't give it up in the end. It's got morphine in it, you see.

Sidney: And what does it do?

Tony: It paralyzes the nerves so that you can't taste this stuff. (*Hands him another bottle*)

Sidney: (*reads*) 'Nurse Irene MacTavish's Cough Cold and 'Flu Elixir'.

Tony: That works in conjunction with this (*picks up a box of pills*), which helps to augment half a dozen of these (*picks up another box*), which leaves the way clear for these to have a bash (*picks up another box*), which strengthen the action of these (*picks up another box*), which sets things up for this to make the final kill (*picks up a bottle*). And if you've still got a cold after all that . . . (*Opens a drawer and triumphantly produces a small bottle*) There.

Sidney: (*picking it up and reading the label*) 'Two aspirins in a glass of milk.' I don't know, you hypochondriacs are so gullible. Buy anything, you would. Shove it in a blue bottle with some cotton wool stuck in it, and you've got to have it. I think all this rubbish should be banned from human consumption. None of it is any good.

Tony: Oh yes, they are. They're hospital-tested. I've seen them all on television, in the adverts. Miracles worked every night. The diagram of the sore throat, his tonsils throbbing away there, arrows pointing towards them, white rings coming out of them (*does it*) — doing, doing, doing. Then the cough sweet slides down. All the good arrows come piling out of it, knocking seven bells out of all the bad arrows, the rings get smaller and smaller, and it's all gone. Your cough's gone, your broken hairs straighten up again, your head stops pounding, you start handing the chocolates round at a dance, playing tennis, going shopping . . . oh, it's marvellous. I'll be up and about again in no time. (*Sneezes*) Rub some of this on my chest, will you? (*Hands him a box of ointment*)

Sidney: I'm not sticking my fingers in that. Rub your own chest.

Tony: Oh, you are callous. How can you be so offhand in the presence of sickness? I'm an invalid, I require attention and consideration. You should nurse me.

Sidney: Hang on, I'll go and get my lamp lit.

Tony: Very funny.

Sidney: Cor blimey — what a tragedy! You've got a cold, so what have I got to do? Go into mourning and burn a couple of joss sticks? It's a cold, it's nothing, you'll get over it.

Tony: It's all right for you, you never get anything wrong with you. Six colds I've had this year and you don't get a thing. Not a sniffle. It's not fair, I object. Why couldn't we have three each?

Sidney: Oh, I'm going out, I can't stand much more of this.

Tony: That's it, go on, leave me. Leave me here to suffer alone. You'll probably find me gone tomorrow morning. Lying on the floor, rigid, flat on my back with my legs sticking up in the air. Go on, I don't mind, leave me.

Sidney: I'm going to. I'm not stopping here listening to you coughing and sneezing your way round the house, wheezing and sniffing all night long. I'm going out to mix with some nice healthy people for a change.

Tony: You unfeeling brute! You wait till you're ill. Don't look for any sympathy from me.

Sidney: (*putting his hat and coat on*) You're not coming to the dance, then?

Tony: Do I look in any fit state to go to a dance? I'd be a big success like this, wouldn't I? I can just see the birds snuggling up close and swooning with ecstasy at the intoxicating smell of camphorated oil coming up through my T-shirt. Do have a bit of sense, Sid, please.

Sidney: Oh well, I'm going, then. Have a nice time.

(*Tony picks up a bottle to throw at him. Sidney leaves quickly. Tony suddenly sees the label. Reacts with surprise when he realizes he hasn't tried this one*)

Tony: 'Dr Wilbur's Medicated Lung Balsam'. (*He tastes it, and reacts with a look of approval*) Hmm . . . 1953, I think. . .

* * *

SCENE 2

The living-room, next day. Sidney and Tony are seated on either side of the fireplace facing each other. Tony is still wrapped up. Sidney is reading a magazine and holding an aerosol room spray. He is wearing a surgical mask. Tony coughs. Sidney immediately sprays the room. Tony glares at him. After a while Tony coughs again. Sidney immediately sprays again. Pause. Tony coughs once. Sidney sprays once. They both glare at each other. Tony begins to wind up for a sneeze. Sidney picks up the spray in readiness. The sneeze dies away. Sidney relaxes. Tony winds up again. Sidney gets the spray ready. The sneeze dies away. Sidney relaxes again. Tony sneezes quickly. Sidney is too late with the spray.

Tony: Har, har, got you!

Sidney: (*taking off his mask*) Do you have to keep coughing?

Tony: How can I stop coughing, it's that thing that's making me cough — that crop sprayer you've got there. How can a man help coughing when there's great clouds of perfumed insect-killer irritating his nasal linings?

Sidney: Its hygienic.

Tony: It's horrible. It smells like a Peruvian dosshouse in here.

Sidney: Well, I'm not stopping till you stop coughing.

Tony: I've told you, it's that stuff.

Sidney: Well, it doesn't make me cough. It doesn't irritate my nose.

Tony: I'm not surprised with that thing. Nothing would irritate that. All the feeling was battered out of that years ago. That's not a nose any more. There's no muscles in there, no valves, no mechanism. You haven't got any control over that whatsoever. It's just a straightforward head ventilator. The wind goes up one side and down the other . . . nothing to do with you at all. (*Taps his own nose*) This is different. This is a delicate instrument. I can pick up Evening in Paris at twenty-five yards with this.

Sidney: Well, it's protecting me against your germs. If you're going to keep on polluting the atmosphere, I'm going to defend myself.

Tony: Defend yourself, yes. But you didn't have to burn all my bedclothes this morning. I've got a cold, mate — it isn't the Plague of London. It's a wonder you haven't got a yellow cross painted on the door. You'll have a bell hanging round my neck soon. Keep away, keep away, the plague, the plague. Take to the hills, Hancock's on the streets (*Sniffs a bit*) I've got a headache now. (*Pause. Clears throat. Immediately Sidney sprays*)

Tony: (*angry*) Oh, stone me, I was only clearing my throat. (*Starts spluttering*) You've set me off again now. (*Coughs away*)

(*Sidney gets up and sprays all round the room while Tony splutters. Tony seizes it from him and stamps on it*)

Tony: (*recovering his breath*) Oh dear. If you bring another one of those things in here, I'll murder you. (*Sidney puts his mask back on*) Oh cor . . . what about the rubber gloves and the white wellingtons, then? Go on, do it properly. (*He sinks back into his chair*) Oh dear, doesn't a cold make you feel miserable? (*Takes a pastille out of a tin and sucks it*) I'll have to get some blackcurrant pastilles. (*Groans*) Makes you so depressed, doesn't it? I've got a head like a balloon here. Oh, I wish I was dead.

(*Sidney mumbles something behind his mask*)

Tony: What did you say?

Sidney: (*taking his mask off*) So do I.

(*He puts the mask back quickly. Tony reacts. Pause. Suddenly Tony puts his hand to his throat*)

Tony: Hallo. (*Feels his throat*) I thought so. Here it comes. Yes, the tonsils are coming up. I thought as much. I'm in for the full lot this time. It's strange, the legs haven't started going yet. They usually start before the tonsils, they've switched round this time. Hallo. There they go. (*Feels his legs*) Yes, they're off. They're softening up. This is the crucial period now. The crisis is upon us. Either I'll start getting better or I've had it. It'll be the shivers down the back tomorrow, the hot and cold waves at five second intervals. (*Tries to stand up*) Hallo, the aches have set in. (*Feels himself all over*) I'm going fast now. (*Goes dizzy. Holds on to the mantelpiece*) The dizzy spells. Oh dear, that was a bad one. Quick . . . (*Points to the wall*) Is that the ceiling?

Sidney: No, that's the wall.

Tony: That's it, then — galloping 'flu, I think you'd better call Mrs Crevatte in.

Sidney: You're not going to let her try out her old wives' cures on you? Her and her sister — the Witches of Salem

Tony: Don't mock things you don't understand. She's had marvellous results, that woman. Even the vicar had her in. Cured his arthritis in no time. A sprig of mistletoe tied round his leg, a raw onion in his pocket, and he was up that pulpit three steps at a time. Tell her to come round and have her herbs ready. (*He totters to the door*) Oooh . . . my back's seizing up. I don't think I've got much longer, I won't last the night, I've had it.

(*He goes out, coughing weakly. Sidney sprays the room with another aerosol can*)

SCENE 3
Tony's bedroom. He is sitting up in bed coughing and groaning, swathed in clothes, four eiderdowns, a scarf round his neck. He takes a thermometer out of his mouth and looks at it. An expression of horror crosses his face. He looks at it again to make sure.

Tony: (*horrified*) No. No. It can't be — it can't be. (*He shakes it down and looks at it again, relieved*) Phew, that's better. That had me worried for a minute. (*Looks at it again*) Eighty-three point two, that's more like it.

(*The door opens and Sidney comes in*)

82

Sidney: Madame Arcati is here.

(*Mrs Crevatte walks in. She is a weird old girl. Not sinister but eccentric. She is carrying a big bag*)

Tony: Hallo, Mrs Crevatte. You got here just in time. I'm a very sick man.

Mrs Crevatte: Don't worry, we'll soon have you up and about again. What is wrong with you?

Tony: I've got a very bad cold, and I'm afraid it might develop into something more serious. I've taken my temperature.

Mrs Crevatte: I'm not interested in all that nonsense — medicine, thermometers . . . pah. Put that in your mouth. (*She hands him a twig with a leaf on it*)

Tony: What's this?

Mrs Crevatte: It's a freshly-cut twig from a horse chestnut tree that hasn't produced any conkers for three seasons. If your blood's got the fever the sap will rise.

Tony: But how can you tell if the sap's rising?

Mrs Crevatte: Watch that leaf. If it withers and dies you will follow it within a week.

(*She sticks the twig in his mouth. She turns to get something else out of the bag. Tony quickly takes the twig out, looks at it, shakes it down, and sticks it back in his mouth. Mrs Crevatte turns back and takes the twig and looks at it*)

Mrs Crevatte: Ah . . . good . . . there's still a chance. You must drink a potion to break the fever. Let's see now . . . heavy cold. That'll be the boiled dock leaves, roots of deadly nightshade . . . no, no, that's measles . . . you want four ounces of holly roots, an ounce of crushed pips from the aubergine, an once of dried nettles, mixed with the juice of three handfuls of dandelion buds. The whole to be pounded on marble and boiled in brass. Ooh, and have you got a nutmeg?

Tony: What for?

Mrs Crevatte: My old man's rice pudding — the shops were closed as I came by.

Tony: Never mind about your old man's rice pudding, you concentrate on my cold. Get this potion mixed up so I can get it down me.

Mrs Crevatte: You don't drink it. We place it in a bowl and you inhale it. That's another thing, your bed's facing the wrong way. The rays of the full moon won't get anywhere near you like that.

Tony: The rays of the full moon? What interest are they to me? I've got a cold, not a strange desire to sit out in the garden baying all night.

Mrs Crevatte: The rays of the full moon are invaluable for treating the ague. It's been handed down for centuries. 'Tis clearly writ in the Almanack . . . 'The rays of the moon must pass o'er the bed, if you don't want to die from a cold in the head.'

Tony: I can't quite see them doing it down Harley Street, still I'll have a go. I'm not having the cockerel strangled over my bedclothes, or the live toads sitting in a semi-circle, I'm not having any of that. Let's get that straight.

Mrs Crevatte: (*indignant*) Just what are you inferring? This isn't black magic, you know. This is a bona fide nature cure.

Tony: No, well, I didn't mean anything. . .

Mrs Crevatte: I'm not a witch, you know. . .

Tony: Mrs Crevatte, I assure you I had no intention of suggesting you were . . . the idea of you nipping about on a broomstick is ludicrous. . .

Mrs Crevatte: All the ingredients I am using have genuine healing properties, they were put there for us to use.

Tony: Well, of course they are. . .

Mrs Crevatte: The moon's rays were used by the Druids with great success hundreds of years ago.

Tony: Yes, of course, I didn't mean to. . .

Mrs Crevatte: My family have been doing this sort of thing for generations with not a suggestion of unnatural practices. . .

Tony: I apologise, no offence, I'm sure.

Mrs Crevatte: If you're not satisfied with my methods, I suggest you go elsewhere.

Tony: I'm perfectly satisfied, I had no intention of accusing you of unnatural practices. We'll forget all about the strangled cockerels and get on with the dried nettles.

Mrs Crevatte: All right, then. Let's get the bed moved. (*She moves the bed round so that it is half-facing the windows. She measures up the angle the rays will fall on the bed*) That's better. Now the protective barrier . . . (*She takes a broom made of twigs and brushes an imaginary circle round the bed*) Sweep a circle round and true, stop this cold becoming 'flu.

Tony: Well, that's plain enough, that's the 'flu taken care of. I feel better already.

Mrs Crevatte: (*finishing the circle*) Don't step outside that circle whatever you do. That's there to protect you. Now, we've just got to get rid of the fever and you'll be ready to start mending. (*She steps over the imaginary circle and stands by the bed, making a few passes with her hands*) Are you ready?

Tony: Yes.

Mrs Crevatte: Do you believe in the power of nature to cure all ills?

Tony: Yes, yes.

(*She starts running her hands over his body without touching it, as if she is drawing the cold off. She grabs his head in the crook of one arm and draws off the cold with the other hand, chanting all the while*)

Mrs Crevatte: Cold, cold, go away, come again another day . . . Mr Hancock wants to play, in the meadows far away. . .

Tony: What are you doing?

Mrs Crevatte: I'm drawing it off. (*Carries on drawing it off*) Can't you feel it leaving you? Don't you feel the fever being dragged out of you?

Tony: Yes, yes, I'm getting better, I can feel it . . . it's going. . .

Mrs Crevatte: (*speeding up the movements*) Fever, fever, hear me shout. Ague, ague, come on out. . .

Tony: Oh, the relief, the relief, it's working . . . it's working . . . I don't think we'll need the nettles. . .

Mrs Crevatte: (*getting excited, drawing harder*) It's coming out, there's not much left. . .

(*Suddenly Tony has a bout of coughing. Immediately Mrs Crevatte stops her actions, takes a can of air disinfectant and sprays the room and herself. Tony grabs the spray and hurls it away*)

Tony: Get out! You fraud! You're the same as the rest of them. You don't even believe it yourself.

Mrs Crevatte: Well, *I* don't want to catch your cold.

Tony: You had me all worked up there, I thought I was getting better. You're a charlatan, madam. Get out, go on, hoppit, and take your crushed aubergine pips with you. (*Coughs weakly*) I've had a relapse. I'm worse than I was before.

Mrs Crevatte: Well, it's not my fault. I did my best.

Tony: I'll have the law on you.

Mrs Crevatte: Don't you start saying things like that. I'm a respectable woman, I've had great success with other people. I've got testimonials. I can't help it if you're not in sympathy. Good day to you. (*She has packed up her things and has got to the door. She goes out. Slight pause. She pokes her head round the door*) We could try a mango root under your pillow.

(*Tony goes to throw a vase at her. She ducks out and Tony collapses back on the bed with exhaustion as the effort is too much for him. He coughs weakly, helpless and miserable*)

SCENE 4
Doctor's waiting-room. There is a line of people waiting to see the doctor, all with heavy colds, wrapped in coats and scarves, etc. Tony comes in and sits down. They all start coughing and wheezing. Tony joins in the coughing. They all stop coughing, take out sprays and spray the air around them.

Tony: I've only got a cold, same as you lot, what's the matter with you? (*He picks up a magazine from the table in the middle of the room and starts flipping through it. After a few seconds he turns to the man next to him. He points to the magazine*) I see Lloyd George is dead, then. (*The man ignores him*) How long have you had yours, then?

Man: I beg your pardon?

Tony: Your cold. How long have you had it?

Man: Three days.

Tony: Hah, a beginner. I've had mine a fortnight. Listen to this. (*He coughs and wheezes*) Hear that? You don't get anything like that in three days. It's taken a fortnight to get it like that. Let's hear yours. (*The man is embarrassed*) Come on, come on, don't be shy. (*The man reluctantly coughs for Tony*) No, nothing there. You'll be back at work tomorrow. Your nose is too white. It's when you get a throbber like this you've got to worry. No, I think I can safely say, I am without doubt the worst one here. So I think I ought to go in first.

Man: You wait your turn. I've been here for three-quarters of an hour.

Tony: Oh, well, please yourself. If you want to take the risk.

(*They all turn and look at him at this*)

Man: What risk?

Tony: I think I've got Asian 'flu. (*A bit louder, pointedly*) I'm very infectious, you know. (*Coughs deliberately. They avert their heads and put handkerchiefs up to their faces*) It spreads like wildfire, you know. Yes. Once you've come into contact with the germs, you're sometimes on your back for weeks. (*Coughs deliberately.*

They edge away from him. A couple move towards the door) I'm told the germ's much stronger this year than it was in the other epidemic. *(Coughs again. The two leave quickly, covering their faces with their handkerchiefs as they pass Tony)* It's not only Asian 'flu, of course. I believe there's a touch of the African in there as well. A much stronger class of germ altogether. *(Coughs)*

(They all get up and move slowly towards the door. Tony coughs again. They cover their faces with their handkerchiefs and go out. Tony coughs for the vanguard as if driving them out like a sheepdog. The man loses his nerve and rushes out, leaving Tony in the waiting-room on his own. He moves up to the chair nearest the doctor's door, very pleased with himself. A nurse comes out of the doctor's room. She looks around the empty room)

Nurse: Next, please.

Tony: Thank you very much.

(He goes into the doctor's room and sits down. The doctor is sitting behind his desk with his head in a bowl just like Tony at the opening)

Tony: Doctor, I'm in a terrible state, three weeks now I've had it.

Doctor: *(emerges coughing and sneezing)* I'll be with you in a minute. *(He goes back into the bowl)*

Tony: *(getting up)* I don't think there's much point in staying, really, I mean, under the circumstances. . .

(The doctor emerges again from the bowl)

Doctor: *(heavy with cold)* Ah, that's better. Now, then, what seems to be the trouble?

Tony: I've got a cold.

Doctor: And what do you expect me to do about it?

Tony: Well, stone me, if you can't do anything, who can? I must say I'm very surprised to find you in this state . . . I mean you, a doctor. 'Physician Heal Thyself'. Not a very good advert, is it?

Doctor: I can't help it, I just can't seem to shake it off. . . *(Has a fit of coughing)*

Tony: Oh, good heavens, man . . . here you are, have one of these. *(He offers the doctor a tin of pastilles)*

Doctor: Oh, I haven't tried these. What are they like?

Tony: Very good, you know, for temporary relief.

Doctor: *(trying one)* Oh yes, very pleasant. I've been using these. *(Shows Tony a tin of pastilles)*

Tony: Oh dear me, no, no, no, no, no, no. They're no good. Tear your throat to ribbons, they do.

Doctor: Really?

Tony: Oh, yes. You want to steer clear of those. What else have you been taking?

(The doctor shows him a collection of assorted cold cures, tablets, bottles, etc. Tony sorts through them)

Tony: I've got that one, got that one, that's no good, I don't know how you can drink that stuff, no, that's no good, got that one, what's this one like? 'Dr Fielders Fast 'Flu Fighter'.

Doctor: It hasn't done me any good. *(He sniffs a Benzedrex inhaler)*

Tony: Oh, this is ridiculous. I don't pay ten and threepence a week to come round and get you better. You must have something. There must be some new stuff about. Come on, what have you got in the cupboard? *(He gets up and goes to the drug cupboard)*

Doctor: Come away from there!

Tony: You must have something here. They're experimenting all the time, I've seen them down at Salisbury injecting eggs. You're keeping it back for your private patients — trying to palm us National Health lads off with all the rubbish. I know your type, a second Harry Lime. . . (*He has opened the cupboard and starts searching around amongst the drugs*)

Doctor: Will you come away from that cupboard, there's nothing in there that's any good for colds.

Tony: (*grabbing a bottle*) What's this? I'll have some of this. This'll do.

Doctor: That's morphia.

(*They struggle*)

Tony: That'll do. Put me out of my misery.

Doctor: That won't do your cold any good.

Tony: No, but I won't care, will I? Come on, give me a shot, shove it in. Don't you understand, I've got a cold. . .

Doctor: (*angry*) So have I.

Tony: Well, you have a shot, too.

Doctor: Oh, don't be ridiculous.

Tony: I can't stand much more of it. I've had it for a fortnight.

Doctor: I've had mine longer than that.

Tony: I demand you give me something for my cold.

Doctor: (*angry*) If I had anything don't you think I'd take it myself?

Tony: (*shouts*) There's no need to shout.

Doctor: Come away from that cupboard or I'll call the police.

Tony: I shall report you to the BSA — refusing to render assistance to a dying man.

Doctor: You can have a sniff in my bowl if you like.

Tony: I've got my own bowl.

Doctor: Then there's nothing I can do for you. We've both got to just let Nature take its course. Now, if you don't mind, I've got a splitting headache, and a very bad sore throat, and my legs ache.

Tony: So there's nothing you can suggest?

Doctor: Well, you might try Mrs Crevatte down the road.

Tony: I've tried here. She's hopeless.

Doctor: No, she didn't do any good for me either. (*Takes an onion out of his pocket*) I've been carrying this raw onion about in my pocket for three days now, it hasn't made the slightest bit of difference.

Tony: Did she have the moonbeams across your bed?

Doctor: That's right.

Tony: Drawing it out of you? (*Does the drawing-out actions*)

Doctor: Yes.

Tony: Cor, dear oh dear — your life in their hands! In future all you'll be getting my custom for is cuts and bruises. Good day to you.

(*Tony leaves. The doctor plunges back into his bowl*)

SCENE 5 Tony's living-room. He is sitting at the table picking half-heartedly at his breakfast, coughing and sneezing and worn out.

Tony: Oh dear. It might help if I could taste it. Could be anything. (*Swallows a bit*) Ugh. What is it — scrambled egg or custard — I can't tell. Might as well turn it in.

(*Sidney enters. He has the mask on. He is carrying a circular steel sterilizing receptacle with lid on as used in operating theatres. He puts it on the table*)

Sidney: How did you get on?

Tony: Hopeless. The doctor can't do anything. Mrs Crevatte can't do anything. Nobody can do anything. What a way to live! It's ludicrous. The Edge of the Sixties. They can put a man on the moon, send a rocket half way round Venus, while there's blokes down here who can't taste their scrambled eggs. It's not good enough. First things first, I say. Scientists — I wouldn't sit down at the same table with them.

(*Sidney takes the lid off the receptacle. Steam rises from it. Sidney takes a pair of surgical tongs and dips into the receptacle and lifts out a pair of rubber gloves. He puts them on. He then lifts out with his hands a plate with a cloth over it and puts it on the table*)

Tony: Is all this really necessary?

(*Sidney takes no notice. He lifts out a knife and fork with the tongs. He lifts one corner of the cloth covering the plate, quickly spears a piece of sausage, replaces the cloth quickly, lifts his mask up, puts it in his mouth, quickly replaces the mask and chews the sausage*)

Tony: Have you finished? I mean, you don't want to run the Geiger counter over me? I wouldn't want to pollute society. I don't know why you bother. You never catch colds anyway. I wish I knew how you do it. I'd give anything to be rid of this lot and never get another one. How do you keep free of colds, Sid, what's the secret? What's the difference between you and me?

Sidney: Quite simple. I keep myself fit, keep in condition, build up a resistance against anything. It's the only way if you want to avoid getting colds. You can't go through life with six colds a winter. The body can't stand the strain. They get worse every winter until one day — the final sneeze — you blow yourself out of bed, straight into a box.

Tony: A box!

Sidney: I'll put you on a keep-fit course. You come out with me every morning for a few weeks, I guarantee you'll get rid of that cold, and you'll never get another one as long as you live.

(*Tony turns slowly to face Sidney with a suspicious expression. Sidney puts the mask back on and they stare at each other*)

★ ★ ★

SCENE 6
Tony and Sidney are running along the road in track suits and heavy sweaters. They approach a set of traffic lights. Tony gives the slowing down signal to the traffic behind him. They stop and run on the spot. When the lights change to green, they set off again. Giving the turning right signal, they turn off right.

Sidney is in front and Tony is flagging. Sidney turns and beckons him to hurry up. He waits for Tony to catch up with him and they set off.

Soon we see Sidney sitting on a milestone out in the country, having a smoke. He looks at his watch and up the road, waiting for Tony.

Tony struggles into view. He is in agony. It is painful for him even to put his feet on the ground. Sidney waits for him to come up, then sets off again. A few yards on he stops and waits for Tony. He angrily waves him to get a move on. Tony struggles up to Sidney, and they set off again with Sidney pushing Tony on.

SCENE 7
East Cheam Gymnasium. Tony is sparring with a very good boxer. Tony is swinging haymaking punches which the boxer dodges with complete ease. Tony swings even harder without making contact until he nearly collapses with the effort. He slides down the ropes to a sitting position and Sidney counts him out. Then we see Sidney lifting a set of barbells with ease while Tony is lying on the floor with the barbells across the back of his neck. He beckons to Sidney to 'get the flaming things off' his neck.

Finally, we see them running again. Sidney trots past going like a bomb. There is a pause, then Tony limps past, walking and on the verge of collapse.

SCENE 8
The living-room. Sidney trots in, full of life and flexing himself. He does a few dynamic tension exercises, then sits down at the table.

Sidney: Ah — marvellous. Toned me right up, that has. Let's get into this.
(*He starts tucking in to breakfast with great relish. Tony hobbles in. Groaning and wincing he lowers himself gingerly into a chair, aching in every muscle*)
Sidney: What's wrong with you?
Tony: What's right with me, that's what I want to know.

Sidney: You got rid of your cold, didn't you?

Tony: Oh yes, I got rid of that. That's nothing to what I've got now. I've sprained my wrist, I can't bend my leg, I've got blisters on my feet and I think I've broken my neck.

Sidney: Never satisfied, are you? Always moaning. You're healthier now than you've ever been.

Tony: I know, that's the trouble. I felt much fitter when I was ill. I knew how to cope then, I was used to it. I never knew how well off I was when I had colds. Lying in bed all day long, all wrapped up, the fire going — ah, that was comfort, mate. Now look at me — a wreck of a man.

Sidney: You must be crackers, you don't want to start catching colds again.

Tony: Yes, I do. You can't teach an old dog new tricks. We all have our own way of life, and mine's being completely out of condition. I want my cold back. (*Goes frantic*) I want my cold back. I can't stand being healthy any longer, it's killing me. (*He rushes to the window and opens it. The curtains billow in with the wind. He takes in deep breaths, opening his shirt*)

Tony: Come on, germs, here I am. Come on, all in. (*Whistles as if calling a dog*) Come on, here I am, where are you. It's your old friend Hancock.

Sidney: Close that window, you great. . . (*He winds up for a sneeze and sneezes violently*)

Tony: (*rushing over to him*) That's my cold. I want it! Come on, it's mine! Do that again! Come on, breathe on me! (*Sidney sneezes again*) That's it, well done, keep it up. Come on, let's have you. (*Sidney sneezes again*) And again, come on, don't give up. That's my boy . . . come on, let's all have a bit. (*Sidney sneezes again*) Good lad, come on, spread it around, let's all have a share, don't be greedy. I . . . (*Sneezes*) Got it! That's it, all back to bed! (*Starts collecting all his medicines. Sneezes*) Oh, this is going to be a beauty this time. (*Coughs*) Oh dear oh dear, oh, I feel better already. There's no doubt about it, as Confucius once said, 'If colds are inevitable, lie back and enjoy them'. (*He sneezes*)

The Missing Page

First transmitted on 11 March 1960

The Missing Page featured
SIDNEY JAMES
with
HUGH LLOYD
GEORGE COULOURIS
GORDON PHILLOTT
TOTTI TRUMAN TAYLOR
GIBB McLAUGHLIN
KENNETH KOVE
PEGGYANN CLIFFORD
ALEC BREGONZI
JAMES BULLOCH
JOHN VYVYAN

Produced by DUNCAN WOOD

SCENE 1

East Cheam Public Library. There are a few people searching the shelves, which are all plainly labelled 'FICTION' 'NON-FICTION' 'CRIME' etc. Tony enters. He is carrying a pile of books. He goes up to the librarian's desk and puts the books down in front of him.

Tony: Good morrow, good curator.

Librarian: Oh, it's you. Overdue again. Seven reminders I've sent out to you.

Tony: My dear fellow, one cannot rush one's savouring of the classics of world literature. Rome wasn't built in a day, and its decline and fall can't be read in one.

Librarian: You haven't got Gibbons' *Decline and Fall* there.

Tony: That's got nothing to do with it. I've got *The Love Lives of the Caesars* here, that tells me everything — and between you and me, I'm not surprised it declined and fell after that lot. Kindly shove the cards back in the sockets and give me the tickets.

(*The librarian goes through the books and looks inside the covers*)

Librarian: How have you got all these books? How many tickets have you got?

Tony: Two fiction and two non-fiction.

Librarian: That's four tickets. There's ten books here.

Tony: Yes, well, Dolly was on last time.

Librarian: Do you mean Miss Hargreaves?

Tony: She may be Miss Hargreaves to you, but to people who she reckons, she is Dolly. And to me she is Dolly. And she always lets me have a few over the odds.

Librarian: That's three-and-eight to pay on this lot.

Tony: Three-and-eight! I don't want to buy 'em.

Librarian: Well, don't take so many out if you can't read them all in time. There's other people want to borrow these books, you know.

Tony: I can't think why. A bigger load of old rubbish I haven't clapped my reading glasses on in years.

Librarian: Then why did you take them out?

Tony: Well, there's not much choice in here, is there? I suppose *Lolita's* still out?

Librarian: Yes.

Tony: I thought so.

Librarian: There's twenty-five thousand other books to choose from.

Tony: I've read them all. I've been coming in here since I was six years old. I've read *Biggles Flies East* twenty-seven times, and I'm not wading through it again.

Librarian: *(hands him a leaflet)* There's a list of our new additions. And one book, one ticket. I'm not Dolly.

Tony: My tickets, please.

Librarian: Not till you've paid your fine. Three-and-eight.

Tony: Disgusting . . . they're even taxing learning these days. *(Gets the money out. The librarian is examining a book)*

Librarian: *(points to a page in the book)* Did you do this?

Tony: No, I didn't. I don't like eggs. And you needn't examine the corners of the pages, I don't bend them over. I use bookmarks. I use a piece of ribbon off my chocolate box.

Librarian: Yes, well, take it out. *(Hands him a book with a piece of ribbon sticking out. Tony takes the book, opens it, and all the pages fall out over the floor. The librarian watches this in silence)*

Tony: It's nothing to do with me.

Librarian: You've been folding the books round backwards, haven't you? That's going to cost you another seven-and-six.

Tony: I'm not paying for bad workmanship.

Librarian: Do you know how to read a book?

Tony: Well, of course I do.

Librarian: You hold it like this . . . *(Opens a book and holds it in a reading position)* You rest it in your hand like that. You don't bend it back like this . . . *(Bends it back and all the pages fall out)*

Tony: Touché. Stand by with your date stamping-machine, I shall return.

(He goes over to the bookshelves. There are a few people looking for books, and some sitting down at the reference table. All is quiet. There are big notices reading 'SILENCE' hanging up)

Tony: *(passing the reference table)* Morning.

(The readers look up angrily and shush him)

Tony: Charming. I was only passing the. . .

(All shush)

Tony: Oh, come now, after all. . .

(All shush)

Tony: Yes, but. . .

(All shush. A little man who hasn't been joining in now looks up from his book and shushes all the people who have been shushing)

Tony: Quite right, too. If you must 'Sshhh' don't 'Ssshh' so loud.

Little Man: *(to Tony)* Ssshhh!

Tony: Oh shut up.

(A man standing by the bookshelves turns round and says very loudly)

Man: Quiet, please.

(Everybody turns and shushes him. Tony goes over to the bookshelves. There is a woman choosing a book from the Crime Section. Tony stops and looks at the title. He shakes his head to her, pulls out another book, hands it to her, gives her the thumbs-up, and carries on. He stops a little further away from her and starts examining the titles in the Crime Section. He apparently can't find what he's looking for so he moves on to the next

section, which is marked 'GREEK PHILOSOPHY'. He starts searching for some books. Suddenly he snaps his fingers and beckons. The librarian comes up)

Librarian: Can I help you?

Tony: Yes. I'm looking for Sir Charles Bestead's *Complete History of the Holy Byzantine Empire.*

Librarian: *(impressed)* Oh. You want to borrow it?

Tony: Yes, please.

Librarian: I'm so pleased. We don't get much call for it. I'm so pleased there are still men of culture left. It's a marvellous edition.

Tony: Oh yes, yes, most useful.

Librarian: I do hate to see it neglected.

Tony: Oh, I often borrow it, I find it most helpful.

Librarian: I've misjudged you, haven't I? Is there anything else I can find for you?

Tony: Yes — er — Plato's *Republic*, the *Complete Translation of Homer's Iliad,* and Ulbricht's *Roman Law* — the Wilkinson edition, of course.

Librarian: Of course, very wise choice. You've chosen probably the four best books we have in the library.

Tony: I agree. Have you got them?

Librarian: Of course. I'll get them. *(Goes off)* The first time in four years they've been asked for . . . *(He finds the four volumes. They are huge tomes about six inches thick. He goes back to Tony.)* There we are. It's times like this that make my job worth while.

Tony: Thank you very much, they're the ones.

Librarian: You can have all these on one ticket.

Tony: Thank you, you're most kind. *(He puts them on the floor at the Crime Section. He stands on them, stretches up, and takes down a book from a higher shelf)* Ah, that's the little beauty I'm after. *Lady Don't Fall Backwards. (Steps off the books)* Thank you very much. I won't need those any more for now. Keep them handy, though, they're just the right height.

Librarian: *(picks the books up lovingly. With passion)* You barbarian! You're illiterate, you are, ignorant and illiterate!

(The readers turn on them and shush them loudly)

Tony: You see what you've done now, you've set them off again. Go on, be about your business, you highly-strung fool.

(The librarian goes off in a huff)

Tony: Oh, these beatniks are becoming impossible.

(He turns back to the bookshelves and studies the titles. Puts his reading glasses on. Takes another couple of books. Moves a pile along, revealing Sidney's face looking through from the other side)

Sidney: Hallo.

Tony: Oh, cor! *(Has a turn)* Oh, dear, you frightened the life out of me. What are you doing here?

Sidney: I've come to get some books out.

Tony: Don't give me that! You've never read a book in your life. Run one, yes, but you've never read one.

Sidney: No, straight up, I joined today. I thought I'd have a look and see what it's all about, all this book stuff, so I've come here.

Tony: And straight to the Crime Section. You're trying to get a few ideas, aren't you?

Sidney: Well, you're looking at the Crime Section as well.

Tony: That is neither here nor there. I read thrillers purely as relaxation between the heavy stuff. I find fifty pages of *Dead Dames Don't Talk* the perfect hors-d'oeuvre to an all-night bash at Bertrand Russell.

Sidney: Bertrand Russell? Didn't he write *Kiss the Blood Off My Hands*?

Tony: *Kiss the Blood Off My Hands?* Bertie — of all people? Of course he didn't! That's not his style at all. You're thinking of Aldous Huxley.

Sidney: Well, there's nothing round here . . . Anything round your side?

Tony: There's one or two things that might appeal to you.

Sidney: Hang on.

(*Sidney disappears and comes round the end of the bookshelf and joins Tony*)

Sidney: Let's have a look. (*He selects a book*) What about this one. Smashing cover. (*Laughs raucously*)

(*A reader turns and shushes them*)

Sidney: Who are you shushing? Are you looking for a mouthful of signet rings?

Tony: Sid, please, not in here . . . no bounce-ups on municipal property.

Sidney: Well, I'm not taking that . . . You heard him shushing me, I wasn't doing anything.

Tony: (*whispers*) He's entitled to — you're not supposed to make a noise in a public library.

Sidney: Oh, all right then, but he'd better watch it.

Tony: Yes, all right. Show me the book. (*Looks at it. The following dialogue is in loud whispers*) I've read it.

Sidney: What's it like?

Tony: Not very good. I wouldn't bother.

Sidney: Yeah, but what's it about? What happens?

Tony: Well, you see, this bird is in the room with this bloke when her husband walks in and. . .

(*The readers turn round and shush them. Tony now mimes the action of the book to Sidney, with Sidney reacting appropriately. Tony describes the girl's shape, then a man with big shoulders. He mimes the man kissing her passionately — jumps back — opens a door. He does a melodramatic step into the room as the husband with a melodramatic 'Ha . . . Ha!' The husband has a terrific fight with the lover — strangling each other, etc. Finally the husband draws a gun and shoots the lover several times. He acts the lover doing the death scene then, as the husband, kicks the body and jumps on it. Then he acts the girl, pleading on her knees. He throws her on one side. Has a struggle with the gun. The gun gets forced against her and goes off. Another big death scene, this time as the girl. She dies. The husband is remorseful. He tries to revive her. He jumps up, puts hand to ear, turns round and puts hands up as the police come in the door. Holds out hands for handcuffs. Imitates the judge sitting at the bench. Describes the wig with his hands. He bows to three sides of the court, raps gavel three times. He puts black cap on, then grabs back of his collar to indicate being strung up.*

By now the librarian has come on to the scene and has watched the last half of this pantomime. Tony suddenly realizes he is there and with great embarrassment busies himself collecting some books)

Librarian: What do you think you are doing?

Tony: And just what do you mean by that?

Librarian: This is a library, not the Royal Academy of Dramatic Art. I've been watching you. You've been creating a disturbance ever since you came in here.

Tony: I was merely describing to my friend what his book is about.

Librarian: We get a thousand people a day in here — supposing they all did it? A thousand people in here, gesticulating. We can't have that in a public library.

Tony: I was not gesticulating.

Librarian: You were gesticulating . . . And I've had complaints. It's very distracting. You'd better get your books stamped up and leave.

Sidney: Here, don't you tell me what to do, mate. You're trying it on with the wrong kiddy. Just don't tell me what to do. I'm not the type.

(*One of the readers shushes loudly. Sidney stalks over to the reading table*)

Sidney: Who did that? Come on, who shushed? Who was it? I'll fill him in. Who was it?

Tony: (*restraining him*) Sid, come away. Don't start anything. You're always showing me up. (*To the readers*) I do apologise, it's not his fault, he hates rules and regulations, it's the gipsy in him. Come on, back to your caravan, I'll buy you a new pair of earrings.

(*He escorts the reluctant Sidney over to the counter*)

Librarian: (*has stamped the books and hands them to him*) There's your books. Back in fourteen days, or I shall ask you to turn in your tickets.

Tony: Very well, but I might warn you, the Chairman of the Library Committee happens to be in the same lodge as me, if you know what I mean. (*Makes a Mason's sign*) Once a moose always a moose — just watch it, eh? (*He and Sidney leave the counter*)

Tony: That's frightened him. (*As they go out of the door a woman comes in carrying a book. Tony has a quick look at the title. Then he yells into the library*) Lolita's back!

(*All the people round the reading table, jump up and make a dignified rush to the counter*)

Man: I believe you'll find I'm top of the list. . .

Woman: No, no, I had my name down before it was published.

(*A heated argument breaks out*)

SCENE 2
Tony's living-room. He is engrossed in *Lady Don't Fall Backwards* . He reacts to what he is reading — it is obviously something rather horrific and very tense. He stops and has a drink of water, then carries on reading. Meanwhile Sidney finishes his book and closes it.

Sidney: Well, if that's reading, you can stick it. What a load of old codswallop! *The Stranglers of Bolton* — they should have strangled the bloke who wrote it.

(*Looks at the cover*) Grant Peabody. I ask you, you can't write books with a name like that. . .

Tony: Do you mind? I'm trying to read. Don't interrupt. I'm on the edge of my seat here,

Sidney: Good, is it?

Tony: Good? It's red hot, mate. I hate to think of this sort of book getting in the wrong hands. As soon as I've finished it I'm going to recommend they ban it.

Sidney: As good as that, is it? What's it about, then?

Tony: It's a murder mystery, with loads of girls in it, and they've all fallen for the private eye, and they're all beautiful and they're all rich, and he's got a big white American car. Oh, dear, it's the sort of life you dream about. He's good-looking — quick repartee — judo — marvellous apartment — all the birds. Well, I'm finished with The Saint after this. I'm a Johnny Oxford man now. This is marvellous, twenty-five murders so far — the New York Police don't know what's going on at all — well, the D.A.'s been in to see the Governor, it's political as well, you see, anyway this Jocelyn Knockersbury, a typist at UNO, has been done in and the plans stolen, along with the seating arrangements at the peace conference. Since then another twenty-four have been done in. . .

Sidney: What, all UNO typists?

Tony: Yes, twenty-five of them . . . (*reads a bit more*) Hallo . . . another one's gone. Ooh, what a nasty way to go. Someone poured water over her electric typewriter. Well, this *is* a mystery. Who's behind it all? Who's the murderer? The bloke I suspected is in Salt Lake City, it can't be him. Do you know, I've been wrong on every page so far. Every time I suspect someone, they get killed. I can't wait to get to the end of it . . . It's going to be a complicated ending, this one.

Sidney: Yeah, well, hurry up and finish it, it's getting late. Have a look at the last page.

Tony: You can't do that! It makes the whole thing pointless — you might as well not read it. It's like looking at the next card when you're playing Snap. Do be quiet, I've read the same sentence three times. Hallo, he's found something. It's all right, Johnny knows who did it. He's found a ginger hair on her skirt. He's solved it, he's narrowed his eyes and a little smile has flickered across his face. He always does that when he knows something.

Sidney: Well, come on, then, who did it?

Tony: It'll be on the last page. He always keeps you in suspense till the last page, this bloke. (*Reads on, getting excited*) Yes, I thought so, he's invited everybody into his flat. He always does that. He lashes them up with drinks, lights a cigarette and explains who did it. Then the murderer rushes to the window, slips and falls, hits the pavement, and Johnny Oxford turns round to the guests, finishes his Manhattan and says, 'New York is now a cleaner place to live in.' The End. Turn over, a list of new books and an advert for skinny blokes.

Sidney: If you know what's going to happen every time, why bother to read it?

Tony: Because I don't know who it is who's going to hit the pavement. Now, please keep quiet, Johnny's just starting his summing up, prior to unmasking the murderer. (*He concentrates on the book, making odd noises as he notes the points being made*) Oh, so she was in on it! She said she'd never been to the Mocambo

Club, but she had a book of matches in her handbag. Ah, so that's what put him on to it. That's clever . . . Of course — the trail of footprints in the snow, all made with a size ten left-footed shoe. So it had to be someone who could walk comfortably in two left shoes. That told him it was a small man who had put a big man's shoes on to lay suspicion on somebody else. But he didn't realise that in his hurry he'd put two left shoes on. Well, I never thought of that. I've been waiting for two one-legged twins to turn up.

Sidney: So who did it, then?

Tony: He's coming to it, it's on the last page, I told you that. Here we are . . . (*Reads*) ' "So, Inspector, you can see that the only person who could have done all these murders is the man sitting over there." So saying, Johnny Oxford pointed his finger at . . .' (*He turns the book over to look at the last page. It isn't there*) 'Men, are you skinny, do you have sand kicked in your face, if so' . . . wait a minute, that's not right. (*Feverishly examines the pages*) There's a page missing. The last page is missing! (*He looks on the floor. Looks on the chair where he has been sitting*) Where's the last page? (*To Sid*) What have you done with the last page?

Sidney: I haven't touched it.

Tony: (*looks again at the book*) Well, where is it? It's gone. The solution's on the last page. Oh, this is ridiculous. I'm a bag of tensed-up nerves waiting to see who did it, and this happens. It's enough to drive a man round the twist. I must find that last page.

Sidney: Show me the book. (*He examines the book*) There you are.

Tony: What?

Sidney: See that ragged edge along there? Somebody's torn it out.

Tony: Torn it out?

Sidney: Yeah. They probably lit a fag with it or something.

Tony: Lit a fag? With the last page? They can't do that! There's plenty of other pages. This skinny bloke for a start, he could have gone without any hardship whatsoever. But the last page of a murder mystery — this is sheer unmitigated sadism.

Sidney: Oh well, what's done's done now. That's a mystery in itself, isn't it? Who tore the last page out? I know who did it.

Tony: Who, who?

Sidney: The murderer, so nobody'll know who it was. (*Laughs*)

Tony: Very funny. I've got to find that last page. I must know who did it.

Sidney: Forget about it. It's only a book. Read another one.

Tony: Don't be a fool! How can I read another one with that one still haunting me? (*He is pacing up and down*) The last page, of all pages — what a terrible, nerve-wracking thing to do to a chap. The last page. . .

★ ★ ★

SCENE 3
The bedroom. Tony is now pacing up and down in pyjamas and dressing-gown. Sidney is in his bed asleep. Tony carries on pacing up and down.

Tony: The last page . . . fancy tearing out the last page! How could anybody do a thing like that?

Sidney: (*appearing from under the bedclothes*) Oi! Why don't you turn the light out and go to sleep?

Tony: I want to know who did the murder.

Sidney: And I want to get some sleep. And if you don't turn the light out and stop pacing up and down, there'll be another murder done they don't know who did. Now go to sleep.

(*Tony reluctantly gets into his bed and turns the light out. The room is now in darkness*)

Tony: (*pause*) You were the same when you couldn't think of the name of that bit player in *Wagon Train* yesterday. You were up all night pacing up and down trying to think of it.

Sidney: (*muffled*) Go to sleep.

Tony: (*pause*) I wonder who did it? (*Pause*) I know (*The light goes on and he is sitting upright in bed*) I'll work it out for myself. I'll deduce it. I'll be Johnny Oxford. All the salient points are in the book, it's like a jigsaw puzzle . . . All you have to do is put the pieces together and you've got the solution. You don't need the last page. (*Takes the book*) Let's see now. . .

(*Sidney turns over and covers his head. He is furious. Tony takes a paper and pencil and a notepad*)

Tony: Now, list of characters in order of appearance. This is where my theatrical training comes in. Jocelyn Knockersbury . . . no, she was the first one who was done in . . . Johnny Oxford . . . no, he couldn't have done it. Let's see, how was Jocelyn done? (*Refers to book*) Ah yes, strangled with one of her own nylons. That means whoever did it had access to her stockings. Oh dear, I don't think I'd better pursue that line of enquiry. Freda Wolkinski was asleep in her pull-down bed, when somebody pressed the button, and she flew up into the wall and suffocated. That must have been someone who knew her bed was a pull-down one . . . therefore they must have been familiar with the topography of her boudoir. Hmm, I don't think I'll pursue that line of enquiry. Still — no, no — when you're a sleuth you've got to be prepared to be confronted with the seamy side of life. After all, New York is probably a lot racier than East Cheam. I mustn't let my natural prudery detract me from the work in hand. Now, people associated with her . . . three girlfriends all murdered . . . two boyfriends, one in the Navy in Japan, and one in California with an alibi. Now. . .

(*Sidney's patience is exhausted. He jumps up in bed and snatches the book from Tony's hand*)

Sidney: Will you turn it in and go to sleep!

Tony: Give me my book back. I'm trying to find out who did it.

Sidney: Go to sleep!

Tony: I refuse to go to sleep until I have solved the mystery.

Sidney: Well, I'm not lying here all night listening to you rabbiting away to yourself. I'll tell you who done it.

Tony: How?

Sidney: I'll skip through it and work it out. I know how they go about it. I've been personally involved in many a smart bit of detection. It shouldn't take very long to work out a load of tripe like this. Then perhaps we can all get some kip.

(*Sidney settles back to read the book . . . Time passes. Dawn breaks outside the window. Sidney is nearing the end of the book. He reads the last page and puts it down*)

Tony: Well, who did it?

Sidney: (*annoyed*) How should I know? The last page is missing.

Tony: Well, I know the last page is missing — you said you'd tell me who did it.

Sidney: Well, how did I know it was going to be so complicated? I thought it was going to be a straightforward bash on the nut up a dark alley. (*He lights a cigarette and starts smoking*)

Tony: Oh, well, we'll just have to go to sleep.

Sidney: How can I go to sleep when I don't know who did it?

Tony: No, I know . . . it's so frustrating, isn't it?

Sidney: Let's try and sort it out between us. (*They start pacing up and down*) Now . . . what was the name of that bird who drunk the carbolic milkshake?

Tony: Ah, the fat one.

Sidney: That's her. Now, she's the key, because she knew about all the others. So whoever did her in was the murderer, and she must have known him, and his relationship with the others.

Tony: Yes, so if we can sort out who was nearest to her, we've got him.

Sidney: That's right . . . and that was the personnel manager.

Tony: Yes, of course. It was him. Harry — er — Harry —

Sidney: Belafonte.

Tony: Not now, Sid, no jokes. Harry . . . (*flicks through the pages*) Zimmerman.

Sidney: That's him. Well, that's that solved. Harry Zimmerman.

Tony: Dear oh dear, thank goodness that's solved. I wouldn't have been able to think about anything else if we hadn't found it. Yes, Harry Zimmerman.

(*They climb back into bed*)

Sidney: Yes, perfect, he knew all their background, he knew where they were all living . . . he knew all their habits. . .

Tony: Of course he did, and he had opportunities to do it, he could call round on the pretext of business . . . they wouldn't have suspected him of anything . . . he's the only one who could have done it.

Sidney: Well, that's a relief. He was little, too, that explains the shoe theory. . .

Tony: Yes, it all fits in. Well, well, Harry Zimmerman. Thank goodness for that. Now we can get some sleep. (*He pulls the curtains*) Thanks very much, Sid, I don't know what I would have done if I hadn't found out. Harry Zimmerman . . . of course, it's obvious now you've explained it. Oh well (*yawns*), goodnight.

Sidney: Morning.

Tony: Oh yes. (*Yawns*) Good morning. Harry Zimmerman, eh?

(*They sink beneath the bedclothes. Pause. Suddenly Tony sits bolt upright and throws the bedclothes off*)

Tony: Harry Zimmerman — he was killed in Chapter Three! You buffoon . . . why don't you read the book properly?

(*Sidney looks puzzled*)

SCENE 4 The library. The librarian is at the counter. Tony and Sidney stride in and accost him.

Tony: I demand an explanation!

Librarian: Now what?

Tony: Where is the last page of *Lady Don't Fall Backwards*?

Librarian: At the end of the book, surely.

Tony: Oh, well, that's more like it, I — it is not at the end of the book. Look (*shows him the book*), it has been torn out.

(*The librarian examines the book and sees where the missing page has been torn out*)

Librarian: Did you do this?

Tony: Oh, for crying out . . . if I'd done it, would I have come in here and asked you where it was?

Librarian: Well, you did some very strange things in here yesterday.

Tony: Have a care, my man, you can go too far, you know. Now look here. . . (*All the people round the reading table turn and shush at him*) Don't you lot start. What are you going to do about it, that's what I want to know?

Librarian: I can't do anything about it.

Sidney: Let me deal with him. (*Threateningly*) Now listen, mate, if you place any value on your teeth, you won't be so saucy. (*Shows him his fist*) Twenty-three knockouts in that. I could make it twenty-four — no trouble.

Tony: You want to take notice, one wallop from that, you'll go right through the Autobiographies.

Sidney: Where's the last page?

Librarian: I don't know.

Tony: Well, who did the murder, then?

Librarian: I don't know, I haven't read it.

Tony: It's your book, you should know what they're all about. What sort of librarian are you?

Librarian: I can't read them all.

Tony: Wait a minute — another copy — have you got another copy?

Librarian: No. We only buy one of each.

Tony: Oh, this is ridiculous. . .

(*Sidney goes over to the reading table. It is the same lot who were there the day before, in the same positions*)

Sidney: Oi . . . has anybody here read *Lady Don't Fall Backwards*?

Woman: I beg your pardon?

Sidney: Have you read *Lady Don't Fall Backwards*?

Woman: I . . . I'm afraid I don't read books like that.

Sidney: Don't give me that jazz — you like a bit of spice the same as anybody else. Come on now — who done it?

Woman: Who done . . . who did what?

Sidney: The murders. In *Lady Don't Fall Backwards*. You must have read it.

Woman: I don't know what you're talking about. Please go away, or I — I shall call the police. (*Gets her smelling salts out and has a sniff*)

Sidney: Oh cor. . .

Gentleman: You're a ruffian, sir. An unmitigated bounder.
Little Man: Shhhh.
Gentleman: Don't you shush me, Frobisher.
Little Man: Well, keep quiet, then.
Gentleman: It's this ruffian.
Sidney: All right, all right, forget it. Go back to sleep.
  (*Sidney returns to the counter where Tony and the librarian are still arguing*)
Tony: Are you sure you haven't got another copy?
Librarian: I'm positive.
Tony: Well, what could have happened to the last page? You must see the book
  when it comes in.
Librarian: Perhaps the previous reader knows something about it.
Tony: Of course — that's it! Who had it out last?
Librarian: I don't know.
Tony: Well, have a look then. Really, you're not being very helpful.
Librarian: (*looking in the novel*) Er . . . here we are . . . last taken out, June the
  21st, 1951.
Tony: 1951? Must have been a best-seller, that one.
Librarian: (*referring to his file*) There was a threepenny fine, so we might have a
  record of the person who took it out.
Tony: That's more like it. We're cooking with gas now, man.
Librarian: Pardon?
Tony: Johnny Oxford — in the book — that's what he says. I believe it's employed
  when one is being favourably impressed with the prowess of another chap.
Librarian: I see. (*He gets a card out of his file*) Yes, here it is. Proctor, W., Mr, 'The
  Larches', Oil Drum Lane.
Tony: Oh yes, very salubrious. Thank you very much, I only hope he's still
  there.
Sidney: Oh, do me a favour — nine years ago? He's probably forgotten all about
  it.
Tony: It's a chance we've got to take.
  (*They walk away, Tony comes back*)
Tony: (*secretively*) Is *Lolita* still out?
Librarian: Yes.
Tony: Oh. (*He goes off again with Sidney*)

SCENE 5   Outside 'The Larches', a broken-down Victorian house. Tony and Sidney go up to the door. Tony knocks. The door is opened by a wild-eyed man.

Man: What do you want?
Tony: Mr Proctor, W.?
Man: Yes?
Tony: Oh good. We've come to see you about a book.

Man: Book . . . what book?

Tony: *Lady Don't Fall Backwards.*

    (*The man's face lights up*)

Man: *Lady Don't Fall Backwards*? By D'arcy Sarto?

Tony: That's the one. You remember it?

Man: Of course I remember it. Have you read it?

Tony: Yes, and. . .

Man: (*grabs him*) Who did it? Who did it? I must know who did it. Who did it?

Tony: Have you gone raving mad? I don't know who did it, that's why I'm here, I thought you might know.

Man: How should I know? The last page was torn out.

Tony: Oh cor. (*To Sidney*) Come on, there's no point in staying here.

    (*They turn to go*)

Man: (*frantic*) You can't just go like that. I spent six years trying to find out who done it . . . It's only these last three years I've managed to forget about it, now you come along and start it all up again.

Tony: Yes, well, I'm very sorry. If we find out who did it, we'll come round and let you know.

Man: Where are you going? You can't leave me like this.

Tony: We're going to find the one who had it out before you.

Man: I tried him. He got fed up with it halfway through and didn't finish it.

Sidney: We'll go to the publishers, then.

Man: I went there six years ago. It's out of print, and they haven't got any left.

Tony: Well, there must be a copy in a shop somewhere.

Man: No, all the unsold copies went back to the publishers. They've been pulped. We'll never find out. (*Nearly breaks down*) Never . . . never.

Tony: There, there, don't take on. Don't break now, not after all these years. Johnny Oxford wouldn't, would he? He wouldn't give up and break down.

Man: No, no, that's true. He'd keep going, wouldn't he? He'd find a copy, wouldn't he?

Tony: Of course he would. And so will we.

Sidney: Here — what about the original manuscript?

Man: I never thought of that.

Sidney: Who'd have that, then?

Man: The author.

Tony: D'arcy Sarto. Of course! And even if he hasn't got the manuscript, he'd remember who did it. Come on, let's find out where he lives. (*To man*) Chin up, I think we're nearly at journey's end . . . (*Hand on his shoulder*) As Johnny would tell you if he were here today, 'Stay with it, man.'

(*Sidney and Tony leave. The man draws himself up, keeping his feelings in check. His face is twitching with the emotion*)

SCENE 6 Outside a Georgian terraced house. Tony and Sidney go up to the door.

Tony: Here we are, 44. This is it Sid, at last we'll know. Straight from the horse's mouth. The author himself. (*He rings the doorbell. Rings doorbell again*) Come on, come on. (*He bends down and calls through the letter-box*) Come on, put that pen down. I know you're in there. Come along now, please.
Sidney: (*taps him on the shoulder*) Hancock.
Tony: (*brushing him off*) I'm not giving up now. (*Into the letter-box*) This is most discourteous. Open this door!
Sidney: (*taps him on the shoulder again*) Hancock.
Tony: Do you mind? (*Bangs on the door. Calls through the letter-box*) I'm not going away. I shall wait here, banging and ringing until you do open the door.
Sidney: Well, you'll have to wait a long time.
Tony: Why?
Sidney: Look.
　　(*Sidney indicates an LCC plaque on the wall. The plaque reads as follows: 'D'ARCY SARTO, NOVELIST, LIVED HERE. BORN 1884 DIED 1949.' Tony is completely floored*)
Tony: Dead? The fool! He can't do that to me! No consideration, some people. How am I going to find out who did it now?
Sidney: Let's face it, we're not going to find out. Let's turn it in, I've got other things to do than go chasing round the country after dead authors.
Tony: Never — I'm going to find out if it's the last thing I do. (*Sudden idea*) Wait a minute — of course!
Sidney: Now what?
Tony: The British Museum!
Sidney: He won't be there, they've buried him, I expect. . .
Tony: No, no, not him — the book. The British Museum keeps a copy of every book that's published in this country. Why didn't I think of it before? All we've got to do is to go to the British Museum, borrow the copy, turn to the last page, and there we are. Cab!
　　(*They walk off, Tony waving his walking stick*)

SCENE 7 The British Museum Library. Tony and Sidney are waiting.

Tony: You see, I told you they've got it. There's not a book published they haven't got.
　　(*The British Museum librarian comes in holding a book. He is an old man*)
Librarian: I've found it. I think this is the one you're looking for. (*Blows the dust off it. Shows it to Tony*)
Tony: That's it. That's the one. (*Laughs triumphantly*)
Librarian: Not a very good copy, I'm afraid. A very interesting binding though, they're using a new process of gluing the sheets to the. . .

Tony: (*snatching it from him*) Give us it here! I'm not interested in how they glue it. Oh, these civil servants. It's not mutilated in any way?

Librarian: No, no.

Tony: It's all here?

Librarian: Oh yes, yes, of course.

Tony: I can hardly look. (*Opens the book. Quickly shuts it*) It's there. Page 201. It's there.

Sidney: Well, come on, open it and read it out.

Tony: Yes, of course. (*Opens the book at the penultimate page*) I'll give you three sentences in. ' "So Inspector, you can see that the only person who could have done all the murders is the man sitting over there.' So saying, Johnny Oxford pointed his finger at . . .' (*He turns the book over*) Men, are you skinny? Do you have sand kicked in your face? If so . . .' Where is it? (*Shakes the old man*) Where's the end? Where's the last page? What have you done with it?

(*Sidney has picked up the book as Tony dropped it on the desk*)

Sidney: The last page is here.

Tony: (*lets go the old man*)Where, where?

Sidney: There it is —— there's a Publisher's Note on it. (*Reads*)'At this point Mr D'arcy Sarto's manuscript ends. He died before he could finish the story. We decided to publish it because we thought the countless Johnny Oxford fans throughout the world would like the opportunity of reading what there was of Mr Sarto's last work.'

Tony: (*shattered, he sits down weakly*) So nobody knows.

Librarian: Is there any other book you would like to look at?

Tony: No, thank you. I've finished with books. I'll never read another book as long as I live. There ought to be a law against selling books with no ending. The Chinese had the right idea, start from the back and work your way forward — you wouldn't catch them like that.

Librarian: It's not unusual. Edward Drew. Franz Kafka, they all had unfinished works published.

Tony: Exactly. You never know what you're buying. Well, I'm not going through all that again. No more books for me. I shall take up some other art form. The gramophone, perhaps. Yes, the gramophone. I'll go and buy one.

SCENE 8 The living-room. Tony is just putting the finishing touches to placing a stereo speaker. There is another speaker and a gramophone.

Tony: Now, the chair must be eight feet from the loudspeaker. You've got to be just right with this stereophonic lark. (*Lines up where the chair should be. Paces out eight feet, one foot in front of the other. Sits down*) That's it. I mustn't break the triangle. Two hundred and fifty pounds' worth of equipment here. All set up ready to blast myself out of my chair. (*Sings a bit*) Boom boom boom boom de boom de boom de boom . . . Ha ha, that's it. This is better than whodunnits.

No messing about. You know where you are with this stuff. Two hundred and fifty pounds. All I need now is a gramophone record. Where's Sid got to? It doesn't take this long to buy a record. If he's been down the Hand and Racquet with my last two pounds I'll — I'll —

(*Sidney comes in with a gramophone record wrapped up in a paper bag*)

Tony: About time, too. Have you got it?

Sidney: Yeah, I couldn't get you Beethoven's Fifth. I thought you might like this instead.

(*Hands him the record. Tony takes it out of the cover, puts the cover on the table, looks at the label on the record*)

Tony: Very funny. Very, very funny. SCHUBERT'S UNFINISHED SYMPHONY!

(*He very deliberately breaks the record over Sidney's head and walks off*)

A THRIFTY MAN
IS A
HAPPY MAN

'The Economy Drive', first broadcast 4 September 1959. Sid James
doesn't look as if he agrees with the motto over the empty fireplace *Radio Times*

In 'The Two Murderers' *BBC*

In 'The Missing Page' *Radio Times*

'Twelve Angry Men' *Radio Times*

Now and then: *above* Simpson and Galton and *below* Galton and Simpson *Private collection*

'The Cold': Hancock as the image of long-suffering patient, both on his own and with John Le Mesurier *BBC* and *Radio Times*

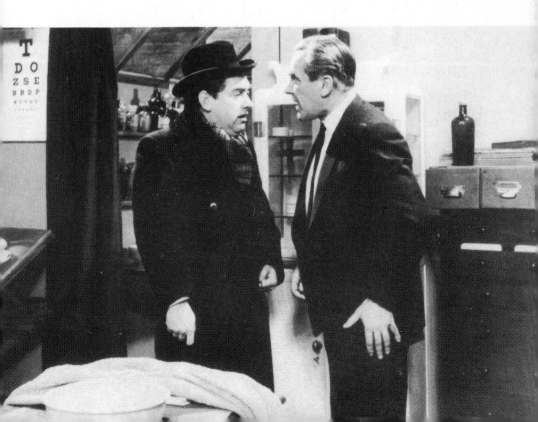

'The Lift' used a simple, but very cramped, s[e]
the entire cast is shown here

'The Radio Ham' had a very elaborate set-u[p]

Radio Tim[es]

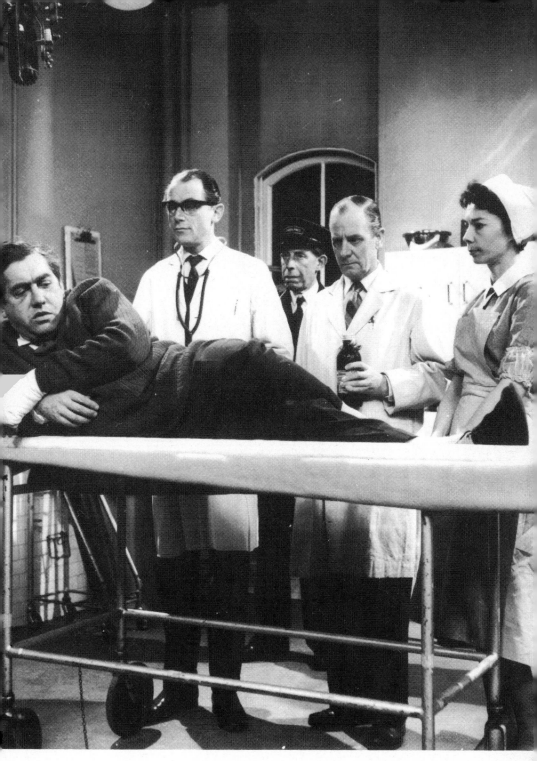

Hancock's most famous half-hour – as a blood donor *Radio Times*

Anthony Aloysius St John Hancock *Radio Times*

The Poison Pen Letters

First transmitted on 6 May 1960

The Poison Pen Letters featured
SIDNEY JAMES
with
JOHN WELSH
PATRICIA HAYES
ANDREW LIEVEN
TOTTIE TRUMAN TAYLOR
ANNA CHURCHER

Produced by DUNCAN WOOD

SCENE 1 Tony's living-room. The table is elegantly set for breakfast: napkins in rings, flowers, etc. Tony enters, very smartly dressed. Humming, he goes to the window, throws it wide open, then sits at the table. Sidney enters in pyjamas and dressing-gown, yawning and scratching himself.

Tony: Good morning. (*Sidney grunts, yawning*) Why don't you get washed and dressed before you come down here in the morning?

Sidney: (*yawning loudly and stretching*) Eh, what's the matter with you?

Tony: Oh nothing, nothing.

Sidney: What's this thing stuck in the middle of me grapefruit?

Tony: That's a cherry.

Sidney: Well, what's it doing there?

Tony: It's an embellishment, that's all.

Sidney: Well, I don't like embellishments first thing in the morning. Either we have a bowlful of cherries or a bowlful of grapefruit, I don't like 'em mucked about.

Tony: What difference does it make to you? You can't see what you're eating first thing in the morning anyway — your eyes don't open until eleven o'clock. You just open your mouth and shovel it in.

Sidney: What are you all poshed up for, anyway?

Tony: I'm not poshed up. This is my normal everyday run-of-the-mill breakfast clobber, as worn by gentlemen the world over. (*Airily*) I shall probably change into something else after I've read *The Times*.

Sidney: You've been to the dentist's again, haven't you?

Tony: How did you know?

Sidney: It's that pre-war copy of *Tailor and Cutter* he's got round there. Every time you have a tooth filled you go round acting like Noël Coward for a fortnight.

Tony: I am merely trying to be civilized. There's a lot to be said for gracious living. Dressing for breakfast is the hallmark of a gentleman. You don't think the Duke of Rutland comes down to breakfast looking like you, do you? Moaning about cherries in his grapefruit? Sitting opposite the Duchess, scratching himself? Let's have a bit of elegance at the breakfast table, please, Sid. Have you finished?

Sidney: Yeah. (*Tony picks up a small bell and rings it. Mrs Crevatte comes in*)

Mrs Crevatte: What do you want?

Tony: You may clear away and bring in the second course, Mrs Crevatte.

Mrs Crevatte: What second course?

Tony: I left the menu out for you — sauté kidneys, lamb chop, bacon, grilled tomatoes and mushrooms.

Mrs Crevatte: You can write out menus all night long, if the stuff ain't out there you've had it, haven't you?

Tony: Are you trying to tell me there's nothing in the larder?

Mrs Crevatte: There's a couple of dodgy-looking eggs, a fly paper, and a mousetrap.

Sidney: Ah, the golden age of elegance.

Tony: Do you mind? Very well, we will have two boiled eggs with brown bread and butter. Soft boiled, three minutes fifteen seconds from the appearance on the surface of the first bubble.

Sidney: And none of your doorsteps. I want them thin enough to poke them in my egg.

Mrs Crevatte: You'll get them as they come off the loaf.

Tony: Please, Sidney, don't upset her, we have enough trouble below stairs as it is. It's very difficult to get staff these days.

Mrs Crevatte: Don't you call me 'staff'. One hour a week I come in here. And you have enough trouble finding the three-and-six for that.

Tony: That will do, Mrs Crevatte.

Mrs Crevatte: And you only have me in so you can tell everyone you've got a woman. I've heard about you down the tennis club.(*Talks posh*) 'Oh, my woman is a perfect treasure, I don't know what I would do without her. You can't find the staff these days, can you?'

Tony: That's quite enough, Mrs Crevatte. Go and put the eggs on.

Mrs Crevatte: They're already on.

Tony: Well, go and bring them in. (*Mrs Crevatte leaves, muttering*)

Mrs Crevatte: Anybody would think we were back in pre-war days. Times have changed, it's us who are going to Monte Carlo these days, not the likes of him. It's us who's got the big cars . . . I think I'll turn it in, it's not worth it. . .
    (*She goes out. Tony picks up* The Times)

Tony: Really, I don't know what the servants are coming to these days . . . Oooh — I see The Hon. Sheila Fortescue is going to marry The Hon. Reggy Hart-Davis. Oh — Lady Pamela Chichester has given birth to a daughter . . . I must send her a card.

Sidney: What's the news?

Tony: That is the news.

Sidney: Inside.

Tony: Oh, I don't know, I never bother. I sometimes have a glance at the Court Circular but that's all.

Sidney: Well, don't hog it all — let's have a look at the dog page.

Tony: The dog page? In *The Times*? Have you taken leave of your senses?

Sidney: All right, all right, give us the gee-gee page, then.

Tony: Oh, take it all, I've read all the important stuff.

Sidney: Oh, cor — why don't you get a decent paper for a change? Why can't we have one with pictures in it? All these words in little print . . . It makes your eyes go funny.

(Mrs Crevatte comes in with boiled eggs on a tray with some letters)

Mrs Crevatte: Here's your post.

Tony: Thank you, Mrs Crevatte. I'll ring when I want you again.

Mrs Crevatte: You'll have to ring a bit hard, mate, I'm off home. I've done my hour.

(She sticks her hand right under his nose. Tony tuts with disgust. He reaches in his pocket and pays her. She counts it)

Tony: It's all there.

Mrs Crevatte: I'm just making sure. I had a two bob bit, a twenty franc piece and an Irish penny last week. Well, I'll be bidding you good morning, then. If you can scrape together another three-and-six, I'll see you next week. And I don't want to find seven days of washing up to do, either. Good day. *(She goes out)*

Tony: She's a misery, that woman. Positively Bolshevik at times.

Sidney: Well, I don't know about that, but she can certainly do an egg all right.

Tony: *(disgusted)* Oh dear, what a way to eat an egg. Well, I'm not going to work on that. She will buy these Hungarian eggs.

Sidney: Well, mine's all right.

Tony: Yours always is. If there's ever two of everything, I get the worst one. It doesn't matter what it is — women, seats, eggs, it's always the same. *(Opens a letter)* Oh, how nice. An invitation to the Vicarage for tea and lantern slides, including a very interesting lecture by the Reverend Mulchrone Waverly on 'The Influence of Gothic Art on the Umboko Tribe of Upper Uganda'. Coming? *(Sidney reacts in disgust)* Well, I think I'll go. You never know when something like that will come in handy in conversation. Suddenly throw it at them, and that's them finished for the evening. *(He opens another letter)* Oh dear, dear, another fan letter. *(Casual)* 'I admire you tremendously, can I have your autograph?' Where would we be without our fans? *(Signs piece of paper)* Yours humbly, Tony Hancock.

Sidney: Humbly!

Tony: Well, I am humbly. I make a point of being humbly. A little bit of humbly never hurt anybody. When you get these letters coming in every day, it makes you realize what a responsibility a man in my position has in the face of such devotion. Look at these, all fan letters . . . all telling me how marvellous I am, the least I can do is to show a bit of humbly. Take this one, for instance — from our own town, Cheam . . . *(reads)* 'Dear Sir, Of all the slimy, untalented, snobbish hypocrites I have ever. . . '

Sidney: Well, what does the rest of it say?

Tony: Mind your own business.

Sidney: No, come on, I want to know what your devoted fans say about you.

Tony: Please, Sidney, this is nothing to laugh at. It's a bit of a shock having that sort of thing sent to you.

Sidney: Aren't you going to read the rest of them?

Tony: No. I don't think I'll bother. I — I'm feeling rather fragile. I — I think I'll go and lie down. Dear me, that's quite upset me, that has. I'll — I'll be in my room if you want me.

(He totters out of the room, Sidney picks up the letter and starts reading it. A few 'Oohs' and 'Aahs' as he comes to some juicy bits)

SCENE 2 The living-room. Tony comes through the door just as Sidney is about to throw a dart at the board chalked on the back of it.

Sidney: Cor, dear, I nearly had you then. Another two seconds and your ear would have been pinned to the door. Hang on a minute. I'm practising for the Darts Championship. Oh, missed.

Tony: I wondered how all those little holes got there. I've been treating it for woodworm for the last six months.

Sidney: Oh, don't keep on, it's only a bit of wood. Now, what's all the fuss?

Tony: Look — I found it on the mat. (*He hands letter to Sidney*)

Sidney: Oh, another one of those poison pen letters.

Tony: The fourth one this week. It's beginning to get me down, Sid, it's playing on my nerves.

Sidney: (*reading the letter*) They're getting better, aren't they? Nice turn of phrase here. They know a lot about you, don't they?

Tony: A bit too much to my mind.

Sidney: Yeah. Don't you recognize the writing?

Tony: No. I've never seen it before. It's someone who's got a nasty, vicious turn of mind, who knows me very well, and who's got a grudge against me. It's you.

Sidney: It's not me. I wouldn't bother to write letters to you. I don't hold grudges — a quick punch up the hooter and it's all over, that's the way I work.

Tony: I can't go on like this, Sid. I'm afraid to come downstairs in the morning in case there's another one waiting for me.

Sidney: Oh, I wouldn't worry about them, it's probably a crank.

Tony: You don't realize what letters like this do to a sensitive man like me. They prey on my mind, I can't sleep at nights. I'm getting to be a nervous wreck.

Sidney: Oh, you're making something out of nothing. Lots of people in your position get poison pen letters sent to them.

Tony: Not letters like this. How would you like to come down to breakfast every morning to find three pages of vitriolic hatred waiting for you on your door-mat? Sid, you know me, you've read those letters. Would you say they were a fair comment on me?

Sidney: Weeeellll. . .

Tony: Well, stone me, if you have to think about it —

Sidney: No, not really, I suppose. I don't suppose you could pin them all together, hand them to you and say 'Tony Hancock, this is your life'. But there are one or two home truths in there, I must admit.

Tony: Well, I'm not perfect, I realize that, we've all got our faults, but surely no one deserves to have that sort of thing hurled through their letter-box.

Sidney: Well, why don't you go to the police about it?

Tony: I should think so! I'm not going to let them read it! You know what a load of gasbags they are. A central sorting office for scandal, that place is. 'I must caution you, anything you say will be taken down and spread all over the town within half an hour.'

Sidney: Well, if you don't do something about it, you're going to keep on getting them, aren't you?

Tony: Oh no, I couldn't stand that. If I get any more of them I'll crack, I know I will. You've got to help me, Sid. We know it's somebody from East Cheam. That's the terrible thing about it. It might be someone I've known for years — a neighbour, somebody I say 'Good morning' to, somebody who says 'Good morning' to me, and 'How's your feet?' and then when I've gone past, stares at me with cold hatred in their eyes.

Sidney: Yeah, I wonder who it is.

Tony: I don't know, but it's very unnerving to know there's someone walking around East Cheam all twisted up with hatred for me.

Sidney: Yeah, and if they hate you that much they might break one day. They won't be content with sending letters, they'll snap and go like wild men. They'll snatch up a chopper, creep into your bedroom one night and take a swing at you.

Tony: Oh, charming, that's all I needed! I'm not setting myself up as a target for some local hatchet man. I've got to find out who this fiend is.

Sidney: The police are your only chance.

Tony: Yes. I'll take a chance. I'd rather have my private life spread all round the town than wake up one morning with my head missing. And I'm certainly not going to bed with a skid lid on every night. Where are those letters?

Sidney: They're in the sideboard drawer, tied up with blue ribbon.

Tony: Tied up with blue ribbon? They're not from Dolly Clackett, you know, they're — They might be! Yes, that's right — no it can't be her. She sent me an Easter egg. Oh, I don't know where I am, Sid. I'll be going around accusing everybody at this rate. Town on Trial.

Sidney: (*getting up and walking out*) Don't worry. The police'll sort it out for you.

Tony: (*following him*) I hope so, Sid. (*Examines holes made by Sidney's darts*) Who's going to believe they're not woodworm holes? (*He goes out*)

SCENE 3 The Police Station. Tony opens the door just as a young constable is aiming a dart at the board hanging behind it. Sidney is following Tony.

Tony: (*ducking*) Oh cor, not you as well. What's this darts mania that's gripped the country all of a sudden?

Sidney: I told you, it's the Darts Championship. We're playing this lot in the First Round. (*To policeman*) I don't reckon your chances, mate.

Tony: Can I have a bit of service round here? (*To constable*) You haven't got any stripes on. Where's the sergeant?

Constable: He's out on a case. What can I do for you?

Tony: You can do nothing for me, young man.

Sidney: He's a copper — what do you expect, Fabian?

Tony: I'm not relating such personal, intimate things to bits of kids who've only just got their helmets. Besides, I wouldn't let young lads read letters like these. How old are you?

Constable: Twenty-three.

Tony: Well, there you are, it's out of the question. He's a mere child.

Sergeant: (*entering*) Anything wrong, constable?

Tony: Ah, authority.

Sergeant: What's the trouble, sir?

Tony: Well, I — er — it's a case of extreme delicacy. I'd be happier if you sent this young lad out of the room.

Sergeant: Oh, all right. Go and sort out the reports in the office. (*The constable goes out*) Now, what's all this about?

Tony: Read those. (*Gives sergeant the letters. The sergeant reads one or two, looking up at Tony from time to time*) Well, don't look at me like that, I didn't do any of those things!

Sergeant: I sincerely hope not. I particularly dislike that bit about putting sixpence on the church plate and taking half a crown change.

Tony: You don't believe that? Me, a personal friend of the vicar — leading bell puller of a Sunday morning? I love that old church. Wasn't it me who slept under those bell ropes during the invasion scare?

Sergeant: It says in there you were hiding.

Tony: Well, I wasn't. I had no reason to hide. When the clarion call came through I was up there with all the other sons of East Cheam, fighting the King's Enemy wherever we found him.

Sergeant: It says in there you didn't go till 1945.

Tony: Yes, well, I was in a reserved occupation. I was working nineteen hours a day making tanks for our lads at the front.

Sergeant: It says there you were making cigarette lighters for the birds in the canteen.

Tony: (*flustered*) Well, they all were — that is, I did my bit, I saw action — I — I don't care what it says there. That's why I'm here, there's nothing but a pack of lies in those letters, and I may add, very offensively put.

Sergeant: And you want us to find out who's writing them?

Tony: Exactly.

Sergeant: Well, someone doesn't like you. It would seem the person isn't very literate, either.

Tony: Oh?

Sergeant: Just here for instance. 'Punch up the throat' — F-R-O-A-T.

Sidney: Oh yeah, he's left the 'E' off the end.

Tony: Are you sure it wasn't you?

Sidney: Of course it wasn't.

Sergeant: Haven't you noticed anything unusual about these envelopes?

Tony: What?

Sergeant: They're all air mail envelopes. See — 'Par Avion'.

Tony: That's French. It's a Frenchman! Of course, that's why he can't spell 'throat'. How many Frenchmen do we know who live in East Cheam?

Sergeant: It doesn't mean he's a Frenchman. They put 'Par Avion' on every air mail envelope. But it does mean that if we can find a postman in East Cheam Post Office who can remember collecting any air mail letters with an East Cheam address on it, we might have something. (*Picks up telephone*) Give me the local Post Office.

Tony: (*to Sidney*) Aren't British policemen wonderful?

Sergeant: Hallo, this is the Police Station. Five letters have been posted recently in your district, all in air mail envelopes and all addressed to 23, Railway Cuttings. Oh, you noticed them. Have you any idea of what box they were collected from? Which one? I see.

Tony: Well?

Sergeant: They were all posted in the letter box outside Number 23, Railway Cuttings.

Tony: Twenty-three . . . (*To Sidney*) It *is* you.

Sidney: It's not me.

Tony: It must be you.

Sidney: If you say that once more *I'll* punch you up the throat. F-R-O-A-T-E.

Tony: (*to sergeant*) Number 23, Railway Cuttings — that's where I live.

Sergeant: Yes, I know. Now we've pin-pointed the area, it shouldn't be too difficult to find out who's writing them.

Tony: (*shattered*) On my own doorstep! Someone from Railway Cuttings! A neighbour. Someone who's watched me grow up from a little boy. All these years I've been nursing a viper in my bosom. Who is it, *who is it?*

Sidney: Railway Cuttings? It's probably all of them, it's a round robin, I expect. Are you sure there's only one signature on it?

Tony: It's the same one each time — 'Yours faithfully, The Phantom Exposer'. What are you going to do about it? I demand you uncover this fiend who is hounding me, this pen dipped in vitriol, it's got to be stopped!

Sergeant: All right, all right, we'll take care of it. We'll come down to your house and keep a watch on the pillar-box. Don't worry any more, we'll soon have the criminal under lock and key.

Tony: And not a shot fired. There's no doubt about it, British policemen *are* wonderful. I'm very grateful, and to show you just how grateful. . . (*Puts coin in charity box*)

Sergeant: Thank you very much, sir. There's a retired old copper somewhere whose life is going to be completely transformed by that sixpence.

Tony: I sincerely hope so. Good day to you. (*He and Sidney go out of the Police Station*)

SCENE 4 The living-room. Tony, Sidney and the sergeant are at the window, watching the letter-box outside. Tony has binoculars.

Sergeant: They don't post many letters round here, do they? Half past four and not one letter has gone in yet.

Sidney: Hang on, there's someone coming. Look, down there.

Tony: It's that woman from Number 5. She's got a letter in her hand.

Sergeant: Is it an air mail envelope?

Tony: I can't see. She's got a big hand. Yes, she's posted it. Make a note of that, Mrs Tribe from Number 5.

Sergeant: Has she got any grudge against you?

Tony: I threw my plimsoll at her Alsatian last week. He was rolling in my radishes. But she wouldn't persecute me over a thing like that, surely.

Sergeant: You know what people are like with animals in this country.

Sidney: Hello, somebody's coming again.

Tony: She looks a bit furtive, doesn't she? Of course — it's *her*. I should have known. The old maid across the road. Did you see the way she posted it? A guilty woman if ever I saw one.

Sergeant: Have you ever crossed her path?

Tony: No, I've never walked up it, either. That's the trouble. She's a spinster, you see. She used to leave her gate open, and smile at me through the window when I went past, but I never took the bait.

Sergeant: Did you ever give her any encouragement?

Tony: Only the normal common courtesies. I used to smile at her and lift my hat. Obviously she read more into that than was intended.

Sidney: And I expect she's seen you walking out with Dolly Clackett, and snogging on the front porch.

Tony: Oh, the poor woman, that must have been terrible for her, seeing her loved one in the arms of another bird. Don't be too hard on her, Sergeant, I too know what it is like to love and be ignored.

Sidney: You more than anybody.

Tony: Do you mind?

Sergeant: Well, we don't know definitely that it's her, there's been another letter posted, and the day's not over yet.

Tony: That's true, we mustn't jump to conclusions, but personally I don't think we need to look any further than her.

Sidney: Wait a minute, wait a minute, look who's coming down the street.

Tony: Mrs Crevatte!

Sidney: Your arch enemy.

Tony: There's a diabolical woman if ever I saw one. Stop at nothing, she wouldn't. She's never liked me.

Sidney: Well, I don't know about the spinster, I reckon it's her.

Sergeant: What do you think?

Tony: Well, she would do it, I've no doubt about that, she'd do it. And she does know more about me than anybody else round here . . . poking her nose in my bureau when she's supposed to be dusting. Yes, she's the one!

Sergeant: What about the spinster?

Tony: Never mind about her, Mrs Crevatte's the one I'm after.

Sergeant: Supposing she didn't do it?

Tony: It doesn't matter, shove her inside as an example.

Sidney: I've just remembered something — it can't be her, she can't write.

Tony: That doesn't matter, she's got a kid at school, she probably gives them to him to do for his homework.

Sergeant: That would of course account for the bad spelling and the child-like writing.

Tony: Of course it does. Go on, bung her inside, nip out and throw a net over her.

Sergeant: We've got to be sure. We have no proof. She is only one of three people who have posted letters in that pillar-box.

Tony: Oh dear, sometimes these democratic safeguards can be a right drag. Look, it's between her, the spinster, and old Mrs Tribe. It's an open and shut case. Lock her up. Give her some dirty great rocks to break up, that'll teach her a lesson.

Sergeant: We'll soon find out. I've got the key to the box here. There'll be three letters in there; if one of them is addressed to you, we'll go along and interview them. They always break down under questioning.

Tony: She won't, you'll have to use the rubber hose on her. I'll go out and cut you a chunk off my lawn sprinkler. . .

Sergeant: That won't be necessary. Come on. (*They go outside to the pillar-box. The sergeant opens it and examines the letters*)

Tony: Well?

Sergeant: There isn't one. Three football pools.

Tony: (*He takes the letters from the sergeant*) Three foot . . . show me! Just when we thought we had them. And I was looking forward to sticking a light in her face and shouting at her.

Sergeant: Come on, it's no good hanging about here. We don't want the writer to see us.

Tony: Now what are we going to do?

Sergeant: We'll just have to keep watch all night. We'll take it in turns, two on and two off, all right? (*He and Sidney go back into the house*)

Tony: Right. (*He examines the letters as he posts them back into the box*) Hallo, Chokers Football Pools. Those are the ones Mrs Crevatte does. (*Tears up her form*) Well, I don't fancy *her* chances this week, anyway. (*He goes back into the house*)

SCENE 5
It is late at night. In the living-room the sergeant has the binoculars trained on the letter-box. In Tony's and Sidney's bedroom, Tony sits up, gets out of bed, and begins sleep-walking. He opens the door and goes out. Sidney wakes and follows him. Tony enters the living-room, sits at the desk, and begins writing.

Sidney: (*whispers to sergeant*) You mustn't wake him up, it's dangerous. (*Reads over Tony's shoulder*) 'Dear Bighead Hancock, I hate you, and everybody down our street hates you. Why don't you turn it in? I saw you tear up poor Mrs Crevatte's football pools, and it's about time the world knew what a nasty piece of work you really are under that snobbish exterior. I hate you. You'll be hearing from me again, yours faithfully, The Phantom Exposer.' So it's him! He's been writing to himself!

Sergeant: Sssshhhh. . .

(*Tony puts letter in an envelope*)

Sidney: An air mail envelope! It was him all the time! But why should he —
Sergeant: Ssshhh. . .
> (*Tony stamps and addresses the envelope. He walks out of the room, closely followed by Sidney and the sergeant. They have to retreat quickly as Tony returns for his hat, puts it on and goes out. Sidney and the sergeant rush to the window and watch him post the letter. He comes back and goes upstairs*)

Sidney: Well, I wouldn't have believed it. Old Hancock writing poison pen letters to himself — it's happened at last. He's gone bonkers.
Sergeant: I don't think so. We've had similar cases before, the psychiatrists say that people often hate themselves subconsciously. There's a conflict between the real them and the outward them.
Sidney: Well, as far as I'm concerned, that's bonkers.
Sergeant: No, no, we've all got these tendencies. It only comes out when we're under a mental strain. Has he been working hard lately?
Sidney: Well, hard for him — a couple of days a week.
Sergeant: Well, that explains it, he's been overworking, things got too much for him, he's got a guilty conscience about himself, and bang — out it comes. The inner him starts writing letters to the other him.
Sidney: Exactly. He's bonkers.
Sergeant: No, he just needs a rest, he'll be all right. Well, there's nothing more I can do. This isn't a police case, you can't prosecute people for writing letters to themselves. I'll leave it with you. Goodnight.
Sidney: Goodnight. (*The sergeant leaves. Sidney starts to go upstairs, then stops*) I'm not going up there again, he's bonkers. (*He goes into the living-room instead*)

SCENE 6 The living-room. Sidney is eating breakfast as Tony comes in.

Tony: Sid, Sid, there's another one come on the mat this morning. Who's doing it — you were watching last night, who is it?
Sidney: Now look, sit down, relax. I've got something to tell you.
Tony: Well, hurry up, I've got to get down to the Police Station.
Sidney: Look — how would you like to go for a nice long rest, on a farm somewhere, right away from it all?
Tony: Really, Sid, this is no time for holidays. I've got to find out who's writing these horrible letters.
Sidney: Yeah, well, that's what I'm coming to. Well. . . how can I put it . . . you see, once upon a time, there was a man. . .
Tony: Oh, cor — fairy stories at this time in the morning!
Sidney: . . . and he'd been overworking, you see. He'd been overworking ever so hard all the year, and the strain got too much for him, so one day. . .
Tony: . . . on his way through a forest he came across a gingerbread cottage, with marzipan chimneys — you great oaf, rambling on there, what's the matter with you? Come to the point, Sid, please.

Sidney: All right, then, you want it straight out — you've been writing those letters to yourself.

Tony: Have you gone stark raving mad?

Sidney: *Me?*

Tony: Writing them to myself — I've never heard anything so ridiculous in all my life.

Sidney: Look, we saw you last night. You've been walking in your sleep.

Tony: (*scoffing*) Walking in my sleep? Really, Sid, you'll have to do better than this.

Sidney: You came down here, sat down at that desk, wrote a letter, put it in one of those air mail envelopes, and went out and posted it. We saw you.

Tony: How ludicrous — why should I write horrible letters like that to myself?

Sidney: Because, as the sergeant said, there's a battle raging inside you between you and your inner self.

Tony: I think I prefer the gingerbread cottage. Look — the writing. See, it's nothing like my writing.

Sidney: You wrote it left-handed.

Tony: I'm right-handed, why should I start writing left-handed?

Sidney: I don't know, perhaps the inner you is left-handed.

Tony: We'll prove this once and for all. Wrote it left-handed, indeed. I shall now explode this fanciful theory. I shall write left-handed and compare it. (*He sits down at desk and does so*) Sid — I'm bonkers — I've gone bonkers.

Sidney: No, you haven't. You'll be all right.

Tony: But why? Why?

Sidney: Apparently you've been overworking. You're all strung up, your nerves are like violin strings. Secretly, underneath it all, you don't like the life you've been living, and your subconscious mind has revolted — you're like everybody else, really, you don't like you either.

Tony: But it will pass, Sid, I will get better?

Sidney: With rest, yes. You just need a break, that's all.

Tony: Yes, yes, I have been flogging it a bit lately, haven't I? I'll move, that's it. I'll change my address then my subconscious won't know where to write to. I'll be right as ninepence in a couple of weeks. (*He dials a number on the telephone*)

Sidney: That's my boy.

Tony: Cheam six? British Railways? Oh all right, I'll hang on. He's probably sweeping the platform. I'll go down to my aunt's farm in Studholme Berkley. What I can't understand, Sid, is you've been working just as hard as me these last few weeks — why hasn't it had any effect on you?

Sidney: Well, you know me, I'm stronger-minded than you, nothing affects me. I just take things as they come. Moronic, I think they call it. What's this?

Tony: Oh, I forgot to give it to you, it's for you.

Sidney: (*reads*) 'Dear Ugly, I hate you, you're a thieving conniving twisting layabout, why don't you do a good day's work for a change, instead of living off other people, you're a parasite, and —' (*He takes up a pen and starts to write with his left hand. He compares the writing with that of the letter, and holds his head in his hands*) I think you'd better make that two tickets to Studholme Berkley.

Tony: Not you as well?

Sidney: Yeah.

Tony: It's amazing we didn't collide on the stairs, you know, in and out of bed all night sleep-walking. It could have been very nasty. What's the matter with them down there? (*Waggles the receiver*) Come on, hurry up, there's two blokes gone bonkers here who want to get away from it all. Go and get packed.

Sidney: Yeah, all right.

Tony: And don't bring your darts. If you start chucking those in your sleep, I've had it. Hallo, Harry, I want two single tickets to Studholme Berkley . . . Yes, singles, I don't think we'll be back for a few months. . .

The Radio Ham

First transmitted on 9 June 1961

The Radio Ham **featured**
ANNIE LEAKE
EDWIN RICHFIELD
MICHAEL PEAKE
BERNARD HUNTER
and the voices of
Andrew Faulds
John Bluthal
Geoffrey Matthews
Geoffrey Lewis
Honor Shepherd

Produced by DUNCAN WOOD

SCENE 1
Tony's living-room. Tony comes in carrying a shopping basket. He switches the light on. He puts the basket on the table and takes out a parcel wrapped in tissue paper. He unwraps the paper and takes out two large radio set valves. He holds them up.

Tony: Now then, where are my radio valves? Aha, you little beauties. We'll soon have you fixed in. We'll soon have the watts throbbing through you, and your filaments glowing red hot, carrying the thoughts and words of mankind to the four corners of the world. Oh, there's nothing like a DS 19/87B. Look at you — a triumph of technological engineering — a work of art. They can keep their Mona Lisa, give me the inside of a wireless set any day.

(*He goes over to one side of the room. All along the wall is built the most complicated transmitting and receiving radio set imaginable. It is tremendously impressive, with many dials, rows of switches, levers, wires, earphones, microphone. On the wall above the apparatus are call cards from all over the world. The wall is covered in them*)

Tony: I bet they're wondering the world over why I've been off the air the last few nights. A radio station like me forced off the air for the sake of fifteen bob, it's ridiculous. (*He puts one of the valves into position, inside the set*) Dear oh dear, seems ages since I had a good old natter with Yokosuji in Tokyo. I wonder how his wife is — what was her name? Er, Radiant Flower of the Divine Heavens. I wonder if her feet are still playing her up. I'm right behind on my transmissions. Who was it picked me up last week? (*Takes a call card down off the wall*) Ah, yes, Rodriguez Dominguin, Rio de Janeiro. I'd better give him a call tonight. I promised to let him know who won the *Daily Herald* Brass Band Competition. Oh, it's a marvellous invention, this is. I don't know what I'd do without this. I'd go crackers. Best five hundred quid's worth I ever spent. Opened up completely new horizons for me. (*Looks up at the cards on the wall*) Friends all over the world. None in this country, but all over the world. Well, ten o'clock. Time I went on the air.

(*He switches on a big mains lever, then a couple of minor circuit levers. He then switches on a panel of six switches one by one in quick succession. Lights start going on as the valves warm up. He tunes in several dials. He then takes two dials one in each hand and tunes them delicately in conjunction with each other as if trying to get some extremely delicate balance. He puts on one earphone to listen to the final adjustment. Satisfied, he puts it down. He then switches on a switch by the loudspeaker*)

Announcer: This is the BBC Home Service. Here is the News.

Tony: Oh, for crying out loud! (*Flicks a switch to cut it out*) I can't get them on my portable. Tune in to Japan, and there they are. (*He fiddles about with some knobs. Finally he is satisfied. He puts his earphones on*) That's better. (*Clears his throat. Into loud speaker*) This is GLK London transmitting on the short wave band on ten point four meters at a frequency of two hundred and fifty megacycles per second. This is GLK London calling HB 24 D Tokyo. GLK London calling HB 24 D Tokyo. Come in, Tokyo. (*He adjusts some dials, then listens intently*) Hallo, hallo, HB 24 D Tokyo. Yoki? How are you? No, no, no, how . . . are . . . you? No . . . how . . . are . . . you? How are you? No, no . . . how are you? (*Tries Japanese accent*) How are you? This London GLK, how getting are you? Oh, never mind, how's the weather out there? No, no, what is the weather like? No, no, is it raining? Raining. Pitter patter. Water. Wet. Ugh, nasty. Hallo, hallo. Yes, listening, go ahead. Sorry, what was that? Yes, I can hear, no understand. I . . . cannot . . . understand. No comprendi. Say it slowly. Slowly. Not so fast. No, no, I can't understand. Can you put it another way? Put it another way. Say it differently. No, in English. Fool! Slowly, now. Slowly. It . . . is . . . are . . . raining . . . not. Oh good, good. Very good. It is are raining not here also. Yes. Cor, this is hard work. Well, what have you been getting up to then? Getting up to? No, no, not when are you getting up — getting up to? What have been doing? Doing. You. What have you been doing? What . . . have . . . you . . . doing . . . been? No, no, no, no, what . . . have . . . what time is it over there? Time. O'clock. Big hand. Little hand. Whereabouts? I know it's not raining, you told me. Start again. Here in London ten o'clock, what time in Tokyo? What time . . . this is GLK London signing off. Goodbye, Tokyo, it's been very nice, same time Monday. Eh? Oh yes. Sayonara.

(*He twists a dial*)

Ah, it's marvellous to be able to converse with people all over the world. People different to yourself, with something new to say, it broadens your outlook, increases your knowledge of things. I bet there's not many people round here who know it's not raining in Tokyo. I suppose I must lead what the social workers call a full life. The world is my oyster . . . I can dip in and have a basinful of anywhere I fancy. Ooh, these headphones don't half make your ears hot . . . (*He takes off his headphones, which have great padded earpieces, and fingers his ear tenderly*) Dear oh dear, like two braised lamb chops under there, they are. I think I'll turn over to the loudspeaker. (*He flicks a switch*)

Now, who shall I have a go at next? Oh dear, Belgrade, I forgot all about him. I haven't spoken to him for six months. (*Twiddles a couple of dials*) GLK London calling HBX Belgrade. GLK London calling HBX Belgrade. Come in, Belgrade. (*He listens as we hear atmospherics through the loudspeaker. Then a voice in a Yugoslavian accent speaks*)

Yugoslavian: This is HBX Belgrade. HBX Belgrade. Yaroslav Mikailovitch speaking. I am receiving you, GLK London. Fraternal greeting, comrade, from the People's Republic of. . .

Tony: Yes, all right, let's get on with it. Are you ready?

Yugoslavian: Yes, I am ready.

(*Tony takes a chessboard with the men fixed into position*)

Tony: King's Pawn to Queen's Bishop Three, check.

Yugoslavian: Ah . . . yes . . . good move. This needs thinking about.

Tony: All right, take your time, give me a call next week. Oh, by the way, thanks for the bottle of Slivovitz.

Yugoslavian: Oh, you received it.

Tony: Yes, very good. I had a sore throat for a fortnight. There's a crate of stout in the post, I hope you like it. Goodbye till next week.
(He twists a dial. Over the loudspeaker we hear an English voice)

English Voice: B45 Malaya calling GLK London.

Tony: GLK London receiving you. Come in, Malaya.

English Voice: Good evening, how are you?

Tony: Very well, thank you. Nice to hear from you again.

English Voice: Are you ready?

Tony: Ready.

English Voice: Your sixpence and up sixpence.
(Tony picks up five cards and has a look at them)

Tony: I'll see you.

English Voice: Full house, kings and sevens.

Tony: What a shame — three aces. How much was it?

English Voice: Twelve-and-six.

Tony: I'll send you a postal order. What's the weather like?

English Voice: Beautiful, not a cloud in the sky.

Tony: Good.

English Voice: What's the weather like over there?

Tony: Perfect, a nice warm night. Oh, incidentally, it's not raining in Tokyo either.

English Voice: Oh good, that'll save me calling him.

Tony: Is there anything I can do for you?

English Voice: Yes. There's something I miss very much, you can't get it out here at all.

Tony: Anything, anything you like. You name it.

English Voice: A tray of bread pudding.

Tony: A tray of bread putting? I can't send that through the post.

English Voice: You can send it by plane, cargo service.

Tony: Oh, all right, I'll get my mother to make you one. Do you want sugar on it?

English Voice: Yes, please.

Tony: Right. Signing off now. Cheers. *(He fiddles with the dial)* GLK London calling CX8 Birmingham. Come in, Birmingham.

Birmingham Voice: This is Birmingham. I am receiving you, come in, London.

Tony: Hallo, Harry.

Birmingham Voice: Hallo, Tone. How are you?

Tony: Fine. Harry, do us a favour, will you? Nip round to my mother's place and ask her to make a bread pudding.

Birmingham Voice: Will do. Are you ready for the game?

Tony: Oh, yes. *(Takes a board down from the top of the radio. Throws a dice from a pot)*

Six. (*Moves a counter*) One, two, three, four, five, six. Up the ladder. Square forty-six. Another go. (*Throws the dice*) Three, one, two, three, down the snake back to square twenty-seven.

Birmingham Voice: Right. I'll have my go tomorrow night.

Tony: How's the weather up there?

Birmingham Voice: Pelting down, it is.

Tony: What a pity. It's not raining in Tokyo.

Birmingham Voice: I know, I've just been speaking to him.

Tony: Good luck to you, he can't even understand me, I don't know how he manages with you. Good night then, Harry.

Birmingham Voice: Good night, Tone.

Tony: Oh . . . tell my mother, sugar on the bread pudding.

Birmingham Voice: Right. Good night.

Tony: Good night. Roger and out. This is GLK London calling all stations. GLK London is closing down and will be off the air for five minutes while he has a quick cough and a drag. (*Switches off*)

(*He gets up from the chair and stretches himself*) Oh, it's very tiring, this broadcasting lark. How they sit up at Broadcasting House all night in their evening dress I do not know. You get all cramped up. (*He does a bit of shadow boxing to loosen up*) Ah, that's better.

(*He lies on the bed. Lights a cigarette. Looks at the packet. In a deep voice*) Dreadnoughts — for men. Get the girl of your choice with a Dreadnought. (*Own voice*) Two-and-seven for twenty. (*He takes a draw and splutters. He stubs out cigarette, gets up and goes over to kitchen*) I think a quick glass of cold milk before we go back on the air. (*He picks up a bottle of milk. Looks at the metal cap on it. There is about an inch missing off the top of the milk*) Hallo, the bluetits have been at the top of the milk again. Look at my gold top, pecked to ribbons it is. They must have beaks like pneumatic drills, some of them. I will not have great feathered heads stuck in my milk bottles, guzzling the cream. It's that landlady. It's her who encourages them round here. Her and her coconut shells and bits of bacon rind hanging all over the place. (*He catches sight of a loaf of bread. It has been nibbled away in bits. He picks it up*) They've been at my farmhouse as well. Look at it, great feetmarks all over it. It's not good enough. Birds have no right to be in towns, why don't they stay in the country where they belong? Wait till they perch on my aerial with a lump of my bread in their mouth — I'll shove a few hundred volts through it, that'll make their feet tingle. (*He cuts himself a chunk of bread, slices off a lump of cheese and puts it on a plate. Pours himself a glass of milk. Takes it all back to the radio, sits down and starts on his supper*)

I wish something exciting would happen. A sort of Race for Life, that's what I want. Whole boatloads of sailors becalmed on the China Seas stricken down with yellow-jack . . . the radio operator slumped over his set, calling in a weak voice for help, and me, the only one who picks up the message, the only one in touch with the stricken victims drifting helplessly in the grip of a monsoon. Inert bodies crumpled over half-eaten dinner, limp legs dangling out of bunks, cabin doors swinging on their hinges, every human being aboard in a deep coma, save for the wireless operator, croaking out messages to me, the only man who can save them. Instead of that all I get is 'Send a tray of bread pudding to Kuala Lumpur'. Oh, well, back to work. Let's have a quick look round the dial, see what's going on.

(*He switches the loudspeaker on. Starts turning the tuning dial slowly. We hear atmospherics, interspersed with snatches of foreign languages, oriental music. Tony keeps turning the dial*)

American Voice: This is the Voice of America broadcasting to the people of Russia. Here follows a discussion on the American way of life.

Tony: I wouldn't bother, mate, they seem quite happy.

(*He carries on turning the dial. More atmospherics, then a snatch of Victor Sylvester's signature tune. Foreign languages. More atmospherics*)

English Voice: Car 35, car 35, report received drinks being served in Three Kings, Agamemnon Road at 11.15. Investigate please. Man beating wife in. . .

Tony: (*makes note*) Three Kings — 11.15pm — that's not bad. I must remember that. (*He carries on turning. Atmospherics. Music*)

Actor: You shouldn't be here, Desdemona, what if he finds us here together?

Actress: I couldn't stay away, Clive, I no longer care what he thinks.

Actor: Oh, my darling.

Actress: Hold me close. I want to stay with you for ever. Oh Clive, Clive. . .

Tony: Oh, cor! (*He carries on turning. Foreign chat, music, in quick succession. A bit of flamenco singing*)

Australian Voice: Flying Doctor calling Fraser Station, I'm on my way, Mrs Fraser. Wrap him up and don't move him. . .

Tony: That's not bad, is it? (*Writes on a pad*) Short wave, eleven point five metres, I'll have a chat with him one night about my backache. (*He carries on turning the dial. A quick melange of languages, symphony orchestra, singing, and atmospherics*)

Yachtsman: (*faintly, getting stronger then fading again against a background of atmospherics*) Mayday. Mayday. Mayday.

Tony: Mayday? What's he talking about? That was three weeks ago. It's nearly June.

Yachtsman: Mayday. Mayday. Mayday.

Tony: Mayday. That's a code word. (*Picks up his book*) It's a code name for a typhoon, isn't it? No, that's girls' names. Alice, Gloria, Elsie. May day. Mayday . . . it rings a bell. Where are we — (*He is flicking through the manual*) Mayday. Emergency. Distress Signal. Help me. (*He puts the book down dramatically*) Yellow-jack! (*He feverishly gets a line on the signal*) Hallo, Mayday . . . Hallo, Mayday . . . I am receiving you. Come in, Mayday.

Yachtsman: (*over cackle*) Thank God you've answered. I've been calling for over six hours. I thought I'd never reach anybody.

Tony: Who are you, where are you located?

Yachtsman: Listen carefully. I cannot keep on the air much longer, my batteries are almost finished. My radio is damaged and I can only transmit on this one wavelength.

Tony: I understand, go ahead.

Yachtsman: Please keep tuned in on this waveband. You are my only contact with the outside world.

Tony: (*drawing himself up with pride*) At last . . . my bread pudding days are over.

Yachtsman: I beg your pardon?

Tony: Nothing. Carry on, I am waiting your instructions.

Yachtsman: Listen carefully. I am the Motor Yacht Billet Doux, out of Sierra Leone. I am holed beneath the water line, and am shipping water fast. I have run out of fuel and am drifting in the Atlantic Ocean three hundred miles off the African Coast . . . I can only keep afloat for another two or three hours. It is imperative you radio for help!

Tony: Roger. Will do. What is your exact position?

Yachtsman: My position is. . .

Tony: Hang on, I haven't got a pencil. Hold on, don't sink yet, I've got one somewhere. I was writing the Flying Doctor's wavelength down just now . . . Hang on . . . ah, here it is. Go ahead.

Yachtsman: My position is longitude. . .

(*Tony presses on the pencil and breaks it*)

Tony: Hang on, I've broken it.

Yachtsman: For heaven's sake hurry, man, this radio can't last much longer.

Tony: Wait a minute, I've got another somewhere. You can never find things when you want them, can you? (*He is looking for his pencil*) What's the weather like out there?

Yachtsman: Oh, for heaven's sake!

Tony: It's not raining in Tokyo. (*He finds pencil*)

Yachtsman: Will you please hurry up, my battery is going fast. My position is longitude. . .

Japanese Voice: How it is weather in San Francisco? It is are raining not here in Tokyo.

Tony: Will you get off the air, you Oriental fool! I've got a bloke here somewhere drifting helplessly with a great hole in his boat. Please keep this wavelength clear. Emergency. Mayday. Mayday. Mayday. Mayday.

Australian Voice: Come in, Mayday. This is Sydney, Australia, am receiving you loud and clear, what's wrong?

Tony: Not me, I've got a Mayday waiting for me to help him.

Australian Voice: You lucky blighter, I've never had a Mayday since I started. Where is he?

Tony: You keep out of this, he's mine. Anyway, I don't know, I've lost him. (*He turns the dial slowly, trying to pin-point the emergency call*) Hallo, Mayday. . . are you receiving me? Come in, Mayday . . . (*Victor Sylvester music*) Get off! Come in, Mayday. Hallo, Mayday, where have you gone? Oh, he's probably drifting about . . . (*Fiddles with the dial*) Why can't he chuck his anchor overboard? How does he expect me to find him if he keeps moving about?

Yachtsman: (*over crackle*) . . . three degrees west. Did you get that?

Tony: Get what?

Yachtsman: My position, I just gave it to you.

Tony: No, no, I lost you, would you mind repeating it?

Yachtsman: Oh, of all the incompetent — Is there anyone else there, this is an emergency.

Tony: No, there isn't anybody else here, I'm quite capable of dealing with it.

Yachtsman: Well, pull yourself together, for heaven's sake.

Tony: Now listen, my good man, don't you take that attitude with me, I'm doing my best. It's not my fault you've got a hole in your boat, you should learn to steer it better, shouldn't you? Now, give me your position again and don't let's have so much of it.

Yachtsman: I'm sorry. Here is my position. . .

(*There is a banging on the door*)

Tony: Hang on, there's somebody at the door.

Yachtsman: (*very angry*) I don't care who's at the door, take my position down! This is a matter of life and death.

(*The banging continues*)

Tony: It's no good, I can't hear you, I'll have to open the door. Hang on, don't go away. (*He goes to the door and opens it. There is a woman in a dressing-gown*) Yes?

Woman: Would you stop playing with that radio of yours? Talking to those silly people all over the place.

Tony: They are not silly people.

Woman: Snakes and ladders, and 'How's the weather?' — I've heard you.

Tony: This is not a snakes and ladders call, madam, this is an emergency. There's a man with a hole in his boat.

Woman: It's his own fault, he shouldn't be out in a boat at this time of night.

Tony: It is not this time of night where he is, it's yesterday afternoon. He is in grave peril.

Yachtsman: Mayday. Mayday. Mayday. Mayday. . .

Tony: Listen to the poor devil . . . now push off.

Woman: If you don't stop, I'll call the police. Let him find someone else to talk to.

Tony: You don't seem to realize the gravity of the situation.

Yachtsman: Mayday. Mayday. Mayday.

Tony: All right, I'm coming.

Woman: You're going to carry on talking to him, then?

Tony: Of course I am.

Woman: Right, I've warned you. I'm going to get the police.

Tony: Good, go and get them, then.

Woman: Insolent man!

(*Tony shuts the door on her*)

Yachtsman: Mayday. Mayday. Mayday.

Tony: I'm coming. (*He hurries back to the set*) I'm with you, carry on.

Yachtsman: (*pleading*) Will you please take my position down and radio for help. Please. Hurry.

Tony: (*whispers*) Would you mind keeping your voice down, the neighbours are complaining. Go on, I'm listening.

Yachtsman: Are you there? I can't hear you.

Tony: I'm whispering.

Yachtsman: I can't hear you. Oh, the man's a maniac, he's gone again.

Tony: (*shouts*) I am not a maniac, I'm whispering.

Yachtsman: That's better. I can just about hear you now.

Tony: What do you mean, you can just about hear me? I'm yelling at the top of my voice.

(*Banging on door*)

Tony: Oh shut up!

Yachtsman: I beg your pardon?

Tony: (*shouts*) Not you . . . her.

Yachtsman: I can't hear you very well. My receiver is fading out, my battery isn't strong enough. Please take my position down, I won't be able to receive you much longer. Here is my position. . .

Tony: Wait a minute, I've lost my pencil again.

Yachtsman: Look, don't bother, I'll throw a bottle over the side with a note in it.

Tony: No, no, go ahead, Mayday.

    (*Loud banging on door*)

Tony: Hang on. (*Slings down the pencil. Stalks to the door. Opens it*) Now listen to me, madam, I've never hit a lady before, but . . . Oh. (*He stops dead as he sees a very large man, many inches taller than him, standing there in his dressing-gown. Behind him is the woman. The man grabs Tony's lapels and forces him back into the room*)

Man: You miserable little worm!

Tony: Now, watch it!

Man: Why don't you belt your noise up at this time of night. I don't like being dragged out of bed once I'm akip.

Tony: I'm not making all that much noise.

Man: No, but she is. She can't get to sleep with you nattering away all night, and when she don't sleep she makes sure I don't sleep. I've got to be up on my crane at eight o'clock in the morning, alert, and wide awake. They don't like it if you start dropping two-ton girders all over the site.

Tony: That's quite reasonable.

Man: Are you going to switch this thing off or not?

Tony: I can't switch it off.

Man: Well, I can.

Yachtsman: Mayday. Mayday. Mayday. Mayday. Mayday. . .

(*The man lets go of Tony and starts pulling out wires all over the place. The radio goes dead. Tony tries to stop him*)

Tony: You fool, leave them alone, you don't know what you're doing. I'm his only chance.

(*The man pushes him aside and finishes pulling the wires out*)

Tony: There . . . you've done it now, haven't you? You have just condemned a man to a watery grave.

Man: And if I have any more trouble from you, I shall take that aerial of yours, wrap it round your neck and hang you out the window. Come, Phyllis.

(*The man and the woman leave*)

Tony: Murderer! Murderer! (*He picks up the loose wires and starts poking them back in. He gets a severe electric shock which makes him jump in agony*) Ooh, it goes right up your arm. (*He carries on sorting the wires out a bit apprehensively*) The fools. I'll never find him again. The poor devil. What a way to go. My first Mayday, and I've failed him. (*He has a wire and is trying to put it in but it won't go anywhere*). Oh, where does this one go? (*He starts tracing the wire along the ground round and round in circles. He traces it across the floor up on to the table and finds it leads to his pop-up toaster. He throws the wire down in impatience. He finishes putting the wires back in and goes back to the radio*) I must find him again. He can't have much time left. Hallo, Mayday . . . Are you still there, Mayday . . . Come in, Mayday.

Yachtsman: Hallo, is that you? This is Mayday.

Tony: Thank heavens you're still alive.

Yachtsman: Now, listen. This might be my last chance of speaking to you. Here is my position: longitude ten degrees thirty-three minutes west, latitude. . .
    (*The radio goes dead and the lights go out*)

Tony: Oh, no! (*He gets up from the set, takes out some change, sorts through it, then goes out into the corridor. He puts the shilling in the meter. The lights and the radio come back on. Tony sits at the radio again*)

Yachtsman: . . . south south east by north north west. Did you get that?

Tony: No.

Yachtsman: Why not?

Tony: I had to go and get a shilling for the meter.

Yachtsman: You're doing this on purpose . . . you want me to drown. You're mad!

Tony: Now calm down, pull yourself together. How can you expect me to help you if you panic? Save your strength, you might be days out there yet. Now, clearly and concisely, give me your position.

Yachtsman: Right.

Tony: Yes?

Yachtsman: Longitude ten degrees thirty-two minutes west, latitude five degrees twenty-two minutes south. Will you repeat that?

Tony: (*reading from the pad*) Latitude ten degrees. . .

Yachtsman: No, no, longitude ten degrees.

Tony: Oh. Longitude ten degrees twenty-two minutes west.

Yachtsman: No, no, thirty-two degrees west.

Tony: No, you're wrong there.

Yachtsman: Look, I know where I am . . . I've got the compass in front of me.

Tony: You said twenty-two degrees west.

Yachtsman: No, no, that was the latitude, five degrees twenty-two minutes south.

Tony: No, no, thirty-two minutes south. I've got it down on my pad. Thirty-two minutes south.

Yachtsman: I didn't say that.

Tony: You did. No, wait a minute, I tell a lie — twenty-two degrees south, you're right. Yes, I can't read my own writing — it's a game, isn't it?

Yachtsman: Look, let's start again.

Tony: Yes, right.

Yachtsman: Longitude ten degrees thirty-two minutes west.

Tony: Longitude ten degrees thirty-two minutes west.

Yachtsman: Correct.

Tony: Now we're getting somewhere, we'll have you out of this in no time at all. Carry on.

Yachtsman: Latitude five degrees. . .
    (*A valve on top of the set blows up in a flash and a cloud of smoke. Then another one goes. Pause. Then a third one. A longer pause, then a couple of bits fall off. Tony sits there and watches all this*)

Tony: (*after a pause*) I wonder if a longitude without a latitude is any good. . .

SCENE 2 It is early morning. Tony is pacing up and down, smoking feverishly

Tony: Half past six. What's happened to him, it can't take three hours to get a few valves.

(*The phone rings. He rushes to it. There is a knock on the door. Tony opens it, to two uniformed squad car members*)

Policeman: Mr Hancock?

Tony: Have you brought the valves?

Policeman: Yes, here they are, sir.

(*Tony grabs them and rushes over to the set and starts fixing them in*)

2nd Policeman: We've been on to Coastal Command, they're standing by. All ships in the area have been alerted. The Inspector said all we need from you is the exact location, and he'd do his best.

Tony: It's nothing to do with him. He's a glory-hunter, he is. I'm the one who's been up all night. I picked the message up. He's just a middle-man.

1st Policeman: Yes, well, let's find the location, shall we? We've all played our part.

Tony: What do you mean, we've all played our part? All you've done is bring the valves here.

2nd Policeman: Get on with it.

(*Tony switches on*)

Tony: This is GLK London calling Mayday. Are you receiving me, Mayday? Come in, Mayday. (*He tunes the dial a bit and listens intently*) No answer. He's gone. Davy Jones has got him. (*One of the constables has taken the morning paper from under Tony's door and is reading it*)

Tony: After all my efforts . . . gone. And we were so close.

2nd Constable: Here, listen to this: Stop press. (*Reads*) 'Dramatic sea rescue. At 4.30 this morning an Englishman was rescued from his sinking yacht by a Royal Navy helicopter from Freetown on the coast of West Africa. The man's radio distress signals had been picked up by a Japanese amateur radio operator. . .'

Tony: Oh no, not 'It is are not raining here also'.

2nd Constable: 'Showing commendable efficiency, the Japanese operator, within seconds of receiving the message, had pin-pointed the exact location and alerted the authorities. "I owe my life to him," said the rescued man.'

1st Constable: Let's get this straight. How come you picked the message up at half past ten last night and you still don't know where he is, and this Japanese bloke picked him up at four o'clock and within half an hour he's rescued?

Tony: Well, I don't suppose he's got a crane driver up above him threatening to duff him up every couple of minutes, for a start.

2nd Constable: Come on, Harry, we'd better get on to Coastal Command and call them off. You want to wake your ideas up, mate.

(*They turn to go*)

1st Constable: By the way, have you got a licence for this?

Tony: Yes, I have.

1st Constable: Hmm, pity.

(*They leave*)

Tony: What a cheek! Up all night, and that's all the thanks I get. Well, that's my Duke of Edinburgh Medal up the spout. Oh dear, what a life.

Birmingham Voice: Calling GLK London.

Tony: GLK London receiving you. Good morning, Harry.

Birmingham Voice: Tony . . . Did you read about that Japanese bloke in the papers this morning?

Tony: Yes, I did.

Birmingham Voice: Good bit of prestige for us operators, isn't it? Makes you feel proud, doesn't it? Sort of brotherhood. By the way, your mum brought the bread pudding round just now.

Tony: Oh, thanks, Harry. Put it in the post, will you? No, send it straight to Kuala Lumpur. I'll tell him it's coming. Cheerio. GLK London calling Malaya. GLK London calling Malaya. Come in Malaya.

   (*Noise of atmospherics. Bit of music*)

Voice: (*over crackle*) Mayday. Mayday. Mayday. Mayday. Am sinking in Indian Ocean. Please get help. Is there anybody receiving me? Come in, please. This is urgent. I haven't much time left.

Tony: Hallo, Mayday. GLK London receiving you. Come in, Mayday.

Voice: Hallo, London, thank heavens you're there. I will give you my exact position: longitude. . .

Tony: Just a minute . . . I wouldn't bother if I were you. I'm not very good at this sort of thing. You'd be much better off with someone else.

Voice: But I'm sinking!

Tony: It'll be much quicker in the long run, I assure you. Good luck. (*He moves the dial*) GLK London calling Malaya. Come in, Malaya.

English Voice: Hallo, London, this is Malaya receiving you. I say, did you hear about that Japanese bloke?

Tony: Yes, I did — your bread pudding's in the post — goodbye. (*He turns a dial*)

Yugoslavian: This is HBK Belgrade calling GLK London.

Tony: Come in, Belgrade.

Yugoslavian: Hello, London — did you hear about that Japanese comrade?

Tony: Yes, yes, yes. We all know about him. Cheerio. (*Goes to tune him out*)

Yugoslavian: Just a minute . . . it's my move. Queen's Pawn to King's Rook Two. Checkmate, I believe.

   (*Tony sweeps all the chessmen on to the floor*)

Yugoslavian: Hello, London — come in, please.

   (*Tony pulls all plugs out of set*)

★ ★ ★

The Lift

First transmitted on 16 June 1961

The Lift featured
COLIN GORDON
JACK WATLING
JOHN LE MESURIER
HUGH LLOYD
CHARLES LLOYD PACK
NOEL HOWLETT
DIANA KING
JOSE READ

Produced by DUNCAN WOOD

SCENE 1 On the top floor of the TV Centre, Mr and Mrs Humphries are waiting for the lift. Mr Humphries is pushing the lift button. He steps back to look at indicator, then goes to stand by Mrs Humphries. There is a pause. The Doctor walks round corner to lift. He pushes the button, then stands back to look at indicator.

Mr Humphries: I've pressed it.
Doctor: Oh. (*He goes over and stands with the Humphries*)
   (*Pause. Tony comes round corner. He goes up to press the lift button*)
Doctor: I've pressed it.
Mr Humphries: So have I.
Tony: Oh well, third time lucky, eh? (*He presses the button, then stands back and looks at indicator. He joins the group*) Good evening. (*They stare coldly at him. Pause. A girl comes round the corner. She presses the button, stands back and looks at indicator, then goes and stands in group. Tony edges up to her*)
Tony: They certainly take their time, these liftmen, don't they? (*There is no reaction from the girl*) They've improved the lifts, but they haven't improved the liftmen, have they? (*Still the girl ignores him*) That's progress for you. (*Pause*) That's the way it goes. (*Pause*) Yes, indeed.
   (*Girl gets fed up, looks at her watch. She presses lift button again, and stands back to see indicator. She returns to group — stands further away from Tony. Tony reacts. A young man comes round corner. He goes up to the group and stands between Tony and girl. Tony reacts. The young man edges up to girl. He looks her up and down. By now Tony has moved in on the other side of her and is eyeing the young man with dislike*)
Producer: (*to girl*) Hallo, I haven't noticed you on this floor before. Are you a visitor or do you work for the old firm?
Secretary: I'm a secretary. I only started this week.
Producer: Oh. Crichton's the name, producer, *Up You Go, Let's Go Dancing*, and *Thursday Magazine*.
   (*Tony reacts in disgust. The girl, however, is impressed*)
Secretary: Oh, really? *Thursday Magazine* is one of my favourite programmes. I always stay in to watch it.
Producer: (*modest*) It's a job. It's not bad — fifteen million viewers — not bad.

When I took it over it only had five. Perhaps we might have the opportunity of working together sometime.

Secretary Oh, I do hope so.

Producer (*moves a fraction closer*) Well, we'll see what we can do, eh?

(*She smiles up at him. Tony is dead niggled*)

Producer: He's taking his time, isn't he? Has anyone pressed the button?

Tony: We all have.

Producer: It doesn't seem to have done much good, does it? Let me have a go.

Tony: He'll come when he's ready, it's no use keep buzzing him.

(*Producer presses the button. The indicator board shows the arrow starting on its arc as the lift comes up*)

Secretary: He's coming up.

Producer: (*cocky*) Yes, I thought he would.

Tony: Well, there's nothing marvellous in that, he didn't know it was your finger on the button.

Producer: There's no need to take that attitude, old man.

Tony: I'm not taking any attitude, I just don't see how you can stand there and take the credit for it. It could just as easily have been me who pressed it, it just happened that he was ready to come up at that particular time.

Producer: Yes, all right, there's no need to make a song and dance about it, old man.

Tony: I'm not making a song and dance about it. I just didn't like your tone of voice, the way you implied that he only comes up because he knows you're here, and that we are nothing.

Producer: Well, let's forget it, shall we, as long as he's coming up that's all that matters.

(*The young man shrugs his shoulders to the girl to imply what a funny man Tony is*)

Tony: Yes . . . well. (*He lapses into silence. He looks up at the indicator board*) Hallo, he's stopped on the fourth floor.

Producer: That's all right, he's picking somebody up.

Tony: Hallo, he's on the move again.

(*The arrow goes to 3 then to 2, and so on to the ground*)

Tony: (*triumphant*) Har, har, he's gone down again, clever dick. I'll say no more.

(*An Air Marshal comes up and joins them*)

Tony: Hallo, an intrepid bird man.

Air Marshal: What's happening? What's wrong? Trouble with the lift? Anybody pressed the button?

Tony: Do you know, we hadn't thought of that. Press the button — you see the military mind . . . Of course we've pressed the button — what do you think we've been doing, trying to pull it up by the rope?

Air Marshal: Well, let me have a go, perhaps you haven't been pushing it hard enough.

Tony: All right, go on then, you have a go. Go on, pretend it's a rocket, you'd enjoy that, wouldn't you? Go on, five, four, three, two, one. . .

(*The Air Marshal presses the button*)

Tony: (*looks up at the board*) No, still on the launching pad. Hard luck.

Air Marshal: Probably mechanical trouble. It *is* automatic.

Tony: Well, yes and no. It's automatic, but to keep up the illusion of full employment, they've got a man in it. Rumour has it he used to be a producer. (*To producer*) If I were you, I'd learn how to work it.

Producer: Are you trying to be offensive, old man? Because if you are, there's the BBC gym downstairs.

Tony: Look sonny, don't show off in front of the young lady, don't push your luck. I may look a mug, but I know how to use myself. (*Clenches his fist*) See this? I don't usually muck about with amateurs, but I'm open to offers.

Doctor: Oh, do be quiet — two grown men behaving in such an idiotic fashion.

Producer: I'm terribly sorry, sir, but this person is deliberately trying to provoke me.

Secretary: Yes, that's quite true. He is. You ought to be ashamed of yourself, a man of your age.

Tony: I am not a man of my age, I'm more a man of his age. I was only trying to defend myself against an unprovoked and premeditated attack from this loud-mouthed yob here.

Producer: I say, I'm not going to stand for that, you've gone too far!

Tony: Oh yes? Come on, then, try your luck — go on, have a go. Here's my nose, hit it. Go on, see how far you get. Come on have a swing. . .

(*A vicar joins the group*)

Vicar: Good evening.

Tony: (*looks at his watch*) Is that the time? The *Epilogue* over already?

Vicar: Is anything wrong?

Tony: No, no, nothing at all, vicar. Just a slight divergence of opinion. Er — good programme tonight?

Vicar: Yes, yes, most satisfactory. My first *Epilogue*. The producer was very pleased. He said I was quite powerful.

Tony: Oh, I am pleased. Oh good, you might do another one, then.

Vicar: Oh, do you really think so?

Tony: Oh yes, yes. Powerful parsons are very hard to come by. What were you working, then?

Vicar: Pardon?

Tony: What did you do, what was the subject?

Vicar: Oh, I was making some observations on the New English Bible.

Tony: Oh, véry good. It gladdens my heart to see the way that's been selling, it really does. I mean, they say we're a pagan country, and it sells like that. It really is most encouraging . . . Do you cop anything out of that, then?

Vicar: Oh no, no.

Tony: Oh, well, never mind, I expect it all goes to a good cause.

Vicar: Yes, I expect so. Has anyone pressed the button?

Tony: Yes, yes, we have. But unfortunately it has all fallen upon stony gound, as they say in the Good Book.

Vicar: Perhaps if I pressed it?

Tony: By all means. An ecclesiastical digit may be just what's required.

(*The vicar presses the button. The indicator board shows that the lift has started rising*)

Tony: (*in awe*) You've done it! By heavens, you've done it! He's on the way up. Congratulations!

Vicar: Oh, it was nothing.

Doctor: Let's wait till he gets here, shall we — remember what happened last time.

(*The indicator board shows the arrow stopping on 7, which is the floor underneath*)

Doctor: See, he's stopped.

Tony: The buzzer can't be working. He's only on the next floor down. Well, I'm not stopping up here all night. I'm going down to the next floor. Anyone coming? Well, suit yourself. (*He goes down the stairs calling as he goes*) Wait for me, I'm coming. Lift — wait for me.

SCENE 2   A few seconds later. The same group of people are still waiting. The lift door opens and the attendant steps out.

Attendant: Going down.

Doctor: About time, too, we've been waiting ages.

Attendant: I'm sorry, sir, slight mechanical trouble.

(*They all file in. The attendant is just about to step back in the lift when Tony comes panting up the stairs*)

Tony: (*staggering*) Hold it! Wait for me! You did that deliberately — you heard me yelling, you deliberately waited till I got there and then shot up here.

Attendant: I beg your pardon, sir, I did nothing of the kind. In any case, if I took notice of all the yelling and screaming that goes on in this building, I'd be up and down all day like a yo-yo.

Doctor: Look, if you don't mind, I have a train to catch — would you kindly get in the lift and let's get down to the ground floor.

(*Tony steps in the lift*)

Attendant: Just a minute.

(*He starts counting the passengers*)

Tony: What are you playing at now?

Attendant: I thought so. I'm afraid you'll have to get out, sir.

Tony: Get out? What for?

Attendant: I assume you can read, sir. (*Points to a notice in the lift*) This lift is constructed to carry eight persons.

Tony: Well?

Attendant: There are nine of us. You'll have to get out and walk.

Tony: I shall do no such thing.

Attendant: I'm afraid you'll have to. You were the last one in.

Tony: That may well be, but I wasn't the last one here. He came after me. (*Points to the young man*)

Attendant: I don't know anything about that. You were the last one in the lift, you'll have to get out.

Tony: Well, I'm not getting out.

THIS LIFT IS CONSTRUCTED TO CARRY 8 PERSONS

Attendant: Well, this lift is not moving until you do get out.

Doctor: Oh, come along, get out, we're in a hurry.

Tony: So am I. That's very nice, isn't it? Take note of this, vicar — Christian charity working at full blast. Now, come along, my good man, be reasonable. One more passenger isn't going to make any difference.

Attendant: They don't put that notice up there for fun, sir. If they had meant nine persons they would have put nine persons.

Tony: But good grief, man, there's room for another six!

Attendant: It's got nothing to do with room, sir, it's a question of weight ratio.

Tony: Are you insinuating that I'm portly?

Attendant: I'm not insinuating anything, sir, I'm just not taking the responsibility. I have a duty to the safety of my passengers; I will not jeopardize their well-being by overloading my lift.

Tony: Oh, the man's a fool. What difference is one more going to make? We might get down a bit quicker, that's all.

Attendant: Eight persons is eight persons, not nine persons.

Tony: Oh, this is the bureaucratic mind gone mad. All right, supposing you *did* have eight persons in here, and they all weighed twenty stone, what then?

Attendant: (*pauses and thinks about it*) Eight persons is eight persons, and we've got nine persons. I'm not moving.

Doctor: Oh, we can't hang about here all night, let him stay in, liftman.

(*The others agree with him*)

Attendant: All right, all right, but I am not taking any responsibility for what

may happen. If this lift plummets like a stone and shatters to pieces on the basement floor, it's nothing to with me. Is that agreed?

(*The others agree*)

Tony: Yes, yes, let's get on with it.

Attendant: Right. Be it on your own heads.

(*The lift doors close. The indicator on the board moves from 6 to 5, from 5 to 4, and stops halfway between 4 and 3*)

SCENE 3   Inside the lift. The attendant is pressing the button.

Tony: Well, come on, what have you stopped it for?

Attendant: I haven't stopped it. It's stuck.

Tony: Of course it's not stuck.

Attendant: It is stuck. (*He presses various buttons*) It's stuck between floors.

Tony: Well, let's go up and start again.

Attendant: It won't go up. It won't go up or down. We're stuck. It's your fault! You great fat lump, it's stuck.

Tony: That's the second reference you've made to my size and I object to it.

Attendant: I shall make a third. You are a great big fat overweight lump and you've made my lift stick.

(*Tony boggles through this, unable to believe his ears*)

Tony: (*amazed*) You have overstepped yourself, sir, I am asking you to step outside and give me satisfaction.

Attendant: (*shouts*) How can we step outside, you great big-headed know-all, we're stuck!

Tony: Will you kindly watch your language? Remember there are ladies present.

Producer: You should have thought of that earlier before you forced your way into the lift.

Tony: Don't you start, sonny Jim. I've had my fill of you. Bits of kids, just out of the cradle, just because they've got their name in the *Radio Times*, they think. . .

Vicar: Now, gentlemen, gentlemen, please, this isn't going to get the lift started.

Tony: Of course, you're quite right, Vic. In the words of my old school song, 'Let's all pull together'. (*To attendant*) Right then, squire, it's all yours.

Attendant: Thank you. Ladies and gentlemen, there is no cause for alarm. I am now going to press the emergency button. This may cause a violent jolting of the cage. It would help to absorb any impact if you were all to bend your legs.

(*The passengers bend their legs, Tony gets down on his haunches. They all brace themselves for the jolt. The attendant presses the emergency button. Nothing happens. They stay bent. The attendant presses the emergency button several times but still nothing happens*)

Attendant: There seems to be something wrong with the emergency button as well. You may all stand up straight again.

(*The passengers stand up but Tony can't get up*)

Producer: Well, really, now what are we going to do?

Doctor: This is too bad. It is imperative that I get out of here — I am a doctor, I have patients to attend to.

Secretary: There must be something you can do.

(*Tony signals the attendant to help him up. The attendant gives him a hand. Tony straightens up, holding his back*)

Tony: Dear oh dear.

Doctor: Vertigo?

Tony: Yes, that's it.

Doctor: Yes. You're overweight, that's your trouble.

Tony: Don't start that, you'll have him off about his nine persons again.

Air Marshal: Well, we seem to have exhausted the mechanical possibilities of getting us out of this, I suggest we all shout for help. Somebody's bound to hear us.

Doctor: Good idea.

Tony: Thank heavens for the military mind in an emergency. Cranwell has triumphed again. Shout for help. Well done. In unison, after four. One, two, three, four.

(*They all shout at the top of their voices for help, conducted by Tony*)

★ ★ ★

SCENE 4
Inside the lift, some time later. Now most of the passengers have given up shouting. The others give intermittent croaks, still conducted by Tony. Tony stops.

Tony: It's no good, it must be soundproof. No one's taken a blind bit of notice.

Attendant: What's the time?

Tony: Half past twelve.

Attendant: Oh well, that's it, then. There's nobody left on duty now. They all lock up and go home at midnight. We're the only people left in the building, do you realize that?

Doctor: Do you mean to say that we've got to wait here until somebody comes on duty in the morning?

Attendant: Yes. Unless we can get the lift started.

Tony: Oh, for crying out loud, we can't stay here till eight o'clock in the morning! We shall be asphyxiated. (*To doctor*) That is the right word, isn't it?

Doctor: Yes.

Tony: I thought it was. What are we going to do? You're in charge, come on, man, think.

Mrs Humphries: Oh dear, I think I'm going to faint.

Tony: You can't, dear, there's no room.

(*Mrs Humphries puts her hand to her face, groans, and swoons up against her husband*)

Doctor: Stand back, stand back, I'm a doctor.

Tony: We know you're a doctor, you've mentioned nothing else since you got here. I can't understand you — I don't go around blabbing about what I am.

Doctor: I think we've all reached an opinion as to what you are, now kindly keep quiet. (*He attends to the woman*) Please stand back, she needs air.

Tony: Take her shoes off.

(*The doctor takes some smelling salts out and she sniffs them. She recovers*)

Doctor: Steady now. You'll be all right, sit down here and take things easily.

(*He sits the woman down on the attendant's stool. She leans up against the wall*)

Tony: (*quietly to the doctor*) Don't worry, I'll keep my eye on her. You can count on me, doctor — proficiency badge in First Aid, Beaver Patrol 11th East Surrey Scouts, and two years behind the goal with the stretcher, Stamford Bridge. I think you'll find you can rely on me in an emergency.

Doctor: I'm not anticipating any emergencies.

Tony: You never know. There are some dodgy people among us. Take him for instance. (*Indicates the producer*) Very suspect. I've seen his type before. All on top, it's all show, nothing in here. (*Pats his stomach*) Crack like a dry stick, he will.

Producer: (*seeing them looking at him and muttering*) I say, are you talking about me?

Tony: No, no, no, it's all right, carry on. (*Quietly to doctor*) See what I mean? Edgy. He'll start twitching in a minute. I've seen it so often, during the war, up in the front line. He'll be shaking within the hour, by half past three he'll be raving bonkers. When he starts going, I recommend a quick belt across the chin. I'll do it now, shall I?

Doctor: No, no. Just keep quiet and everything will be all right.

Mr Humphries: Gentlemen, it occurs to us that perhaps we should appoint someone to take charge, and we thought that the Air Marshal with his vast experience of commanding men in desperate situations is by far the best man for the job.

Tony: He's had his chance — 'All yell for help' — well, he hasn't got my confidence.

Attendant: Now listen, you, if it hadn't been for you we wouldn't be in this mess in the first place.

Tony: It's your incompetent handling of the lift that's done it — putting learners on a complicated piece of mechanism like this — you have no right to be going up and down this hole all day long. You're a menace.

Vicar: Gentlemen, gentlemen, please — we mustn't give way under the strain. Nothing is solved by squabbling amongst ourselves.

(*Tony folds his arms and takes no further part*)

Producer: I agree. Well, Air Marshal, any ideas?

Tony: Huh, this'll be a laugh.

Producer: Please, do you mind?

Tony: I'm terribly sorry.

Producer: Air Marshal?

Air Marshal: Yes, well, the way I see it is, we are in a hole. . .

Tony: Oh, cor!

Air Marshal: And we have got to get out of it. (*A 'Stone me' reaction from Tony*) So . . . what I propose is this. We hack a hole in the roof, two of us climb out, one stands on the other's shoulders, and forces open the doors on the floor above.

Tony: And that's it, is it?

Air Marshal: Yes.

Tony: Brilliant. So if you all will kindly put on your dark goggles the Air Marshal will step forward with his oxyacetylene cutter and have us out of here in no time. You buffoon. It's metal . . . (*bangs the side*) . . . how are you going to hack your way out of that? Dear oh dear, keep the bomb with blokes like him on the button.

Producer: All right, then, perhaps you've got a better idea?

Tony: Yes, I have. Doctor, what have you got in that bag of yours? Have you got any sleeping pills?

Doctor: Yes.

Tony: Right, two each all round and let's forget about it.

Mrs Humphries: No, no, I've got to get out of here! I can't stay in here till morning, I must get out, I'm suffocating, I'm suffocating, I can't stand it in here.

Mr Humphries: My wife has claustrophobia.

Tony: I see. Well, that's a very handy thing to have in a lift, isn't it? (*Laughs*)

Doctor: Would you mind keeping your tasteless remarks to yourself?

Tony: I'm sorry, I was just trying to keep the party going, didn't mean anything.

Doctor: (*going over to Mrs Humphries*) She'll be all right, there's nothing to worry about. (*Gives her some tablets*) Take these, it'll calm you down.

(*She sits down again on the attendant's seat. The girl goes over and comforts her*)

Producer: (*to Tony*) Have you any more brilliant ideas?

Tony: Yes, I have. Circumstances being what they are, I think we should put my second plan into operation.

Producer: Which is?

Tony: We all jump up and down.

Attendant: All jump up and down?

Tony: Well, it's logical. We might get down a bit faster, that's all. But the way she's going, the quicker the better.

Attendant: And supposing the bottom falls out? Supposing the cable snaps? Supposing we hurtle to the bottom of the lift shaft?

Tony: You have hit upon the one weakness of this whole scheme, haven't you? But the bottom won't fall out, surely. I mean, look at it, solidly made . . . the cable is made to take heavy loads . . . the whole structure is a triumph of British engineering and — yes, perhaps you're right, let's have the pills round.

Secretary: Well, I think it's worth trying.

Producer: Well, in that case, so do I.

Air Marshal: Yes, we might give it a go. Anything to get us out of this blasted box.

Tony: Right, we'll do it. Take your cue from me. One, two, three, jump, jump, jump, jump. . .

(*They all jump up and down in unison. Outside the lift, the indicator board shows the arrow suddenly plummet from in between 4 and 3 to halfway between 3 and 2. . .*)

SCENE 5   Inside the lift, some time later. The passengers have relaxed slightly. The men have loosened their collars. They are sitting on the lift floor. A couple are asleep. The secretary is nestled on the young man's shoulder. After a while the doctor looks at his watch.

Doctor: Half past four.

Tony: Of course, this is nothing new to an old submarine man like me. It's just like the old days. Lying on the bottom, engines off, still, silent. Nobody daring to move. Jerry destroyers dashing about upstairs trying to find us sitting there, sweating, waiting, joined together in a common bond of mutual peril. Yes, it's all too familiar.

Vicar: I thought you said earlier you were in the Army?

Tony: Did I? Oh well, yes, I was. I was attached to a Commando Unit being transported by submarines to blow up the heavy water plants in Norway. Very tricky stuff, heavy water, very tricky. Have you ever handled it?

Vicar: No, I can't say I have.

Tony: You don't want to. Very tricky stuff. A cup full of that in your font, blow the roof off, it would. Dear oh dear, it's hot in here, isn't it? Stuffy.

Vicar: Yes, it's in the air.

Tony: Yes. Too many people breathing too little air. It's a funny thing, air. You can't see it, you can't touch it, you can't smell it, but it's there. It's just as well we've got it all around us. I mean, supposing you had to carry your own supply around with you — when you were born they said, 'There you are, there's your lot, drag that around with you' — it would be very awkward. You'd have to have something the size of the Albert Hall. You'd need wide streets and big doorways to get in and out of. It wouldn't work. I reckon the ants would have taken over by now.

Vicar: Fortunately, there is enough air for us all.

Tony: Ah yes, but for how long? I mean, the rate we're multiplying, we're going to use it all up. There'll be a thousand million Chinamen by 1980 and they've all got noses, you know. I reckon in a couple of hundred years' time, you won't be able to move. We'll be standing shoulder to shoulder all over the world, heads up, fighting for breath. The tallest bloke with the biggest hooter survives. That's the way it's going to go. Natural selection. We'll be a race of giants with big hooters. What do you think, doctor?

Doctor: I don't know and I don't care.

Tony: Charming. That's the medical profession for you. Doesn't it concern you that one day all the little blokes with small noses will be wiped out?

Doctor: Well, you've got nothing to worry about, have you?

Tony: Now there's no need to get personal, old man.

Doctor: Well, then, keep quiet and go to sleep. It's bad enough to be in this predicament without having to listen to your inane chatter . . . dragging Albert Halls around with you.

(*After a little pause*)

Tony: (*to vicar*) I didn't think he'd be the first to crack.

Doctor: I've not cracked! I am in full command of my faculties.

Tony: Well, stop twitching, then.

Doctor: I'm not twitching.

Tony: All right, all right. (*Whispers to vicar*). Claustrophobia.

Doctor: I have not got claustrophobia !

Tony: No, no, of course not. Now, calm down. Have a pill.

(*The doctor hides his face in his hands, frustrated at having met such an aggravating man*)

Tony: I've got an idea. Wake up, everybody, come along, wake up, wake up.

(*They all rouse themselves*)

Air Marshal: Eh? What's wrong, what's happening?

Tony: We're going to play some games.

Air Marshal: Oh, really!

Tony: Keep your minds off the danger. The doctor's not well, we've got to cheer him up.

Doctor: (*helpless*) I'm perfectly all right.

Tony: Yes, yes, of course you are, you're lovely. You'll enjoy this. Ideal game for when you're stuck in a lift. Now, I start. I think of a well-known film, book, play or song. I act the title out and you have to guess what it is.

Producer: Sounds rather childish.

Tony: Right up your street, then. (*Laughs*) Right, here we go.

(*Tony starts cranking an imaginary camera. The Air Marshal and the doctor look at him and each other in disdain*)

Secretary: It's a film.

Tony: Yes, yes — see, she's got the idea. Now . . . (*He does the proscenium arch. He does it again*)

Secretary: It's a play as well.

Tony: Yes. Now here's the main bit. (*He holds his hand up and peers into the distance. Turns and looks behind him. Pulls a pint and drinks it. Stamps his foot and waves his arms*)

Producer: *Look Back In Anger.*

Tony: Well, give us a chance!

Producer: It was simple.

Secretary: How clever of you, how did you work that out?

Tony: It wasn't clever. I gave you a very easy one to start everybody off. Look . . . (*does it*). Back (*turns round*). In (*pulls pint and drinks it*) — pub, see — clever, that was — Anger (*stamps his foot*).

Attendant: Don't do that, you know what happened last time.

Tony: I'll make this one harder. (*He cranks imaginary camera*)

Secretary: A film.

(*Tony points to his eye. Washes his face and hands. Draws an 'H' and cuts round it with scissors. Takes it out, rolls it up and throws it away, struts up and down like a teenager, chewing gum, etc. Uses two index fingers to imitate fangs and then howls*)

Producer: (*uninterested*). *I Was A Teenage Werewolf.*

Tony: Oh.

Secretary: Was he right, then?

Tony: Of course he was right.

Secretary: How clever. It's your turn now.

Producer: I don't want to play the stupid game.

Tony: If you don't want to play, stop guessing them, then.

Air Marshal: Just a minute, I'm not the slightest bit interested in this nonsense, but how did you make 'was'?

Tony: This (*washes his hands and face*) — Wash. You don't want the 'H' (*draws an 'H' in the air*) so you cut round it (*cuts round it. Takes it out, rolls it up and throws it away*). Take it out, roll it up and throw it away.

Air Marshal: Oh, really?

Tony: Here you are, here's one. (*He pretends to sing an operatic aria*).

Secretary: A song title.

(*Tony pretends to open a box of chocolates, picks one out, pops it in his mouth, chews and looks very pleased. Then he does a guardsman going through his sentry routine*)

Producer: *The Chocolate Soldier.*

Tony: I hadn't finished!

Producer: Well, it was, wasn't it?

Tony: Yes, and I'm not playing any more.

Air Marshal: Good, now perhaps we can get some sleep.

Tony: Sleep? We're coming out of this lift singing, mate. There'll be newsreel cameras out there waiting for us — we'll show them how the British behave when they're up against it. Altogether now — I'll be Alec Guinness. (*He starts whistling 'Colonel Bogey', urging them on. They join in reluctantly one by one*) Well, come on, then.

SCENE 6
Some hours later, inside the lift. They are all singing 'Pack up your troubles in your old kit bag'. All,
that is, except Tony, who is fast asleep. The vicar is
conducting. Suddenly there is tapping from outside
the lift.

Vicar: Quiet — listen.
  (*More tapping*)
Fireman 1: Are you all right in there?
Vicar: Yes, we're all well.
Fireman 1: We'll soon have you out. Hold on.
Mrs Humphries: We're saved! We're saved! (*She shakes Tony*) Wake up, we're saved!
  (*Tony comes to and starts whistling 'Colonel Bogey'*)
Tony: Well, come on then. . . (*whistles*)
Air Marshal: That was hours ago.
Tony: Was it? Oh. I must have dropped off for five minutes. What's happening, then?
Vicar: They've found us. We'll be getting out any minute now. Look.
  (*A crowbar comes through the doors and forces them open, then two hands come through and open the doors right out, revealing two firemen. The firemen help them out on to the landing. They get to Tony*)
Fireman 2: Are you all right, sir?
Tony: Yes, thank you. Well done, lads. Where are the cameras?
  (*The firemen help out the others. A man walks over to the group*)
Man: I am the Chief Engineer of the BBC Maintenance Department. I apologise on behalf of the Corporation for what has happened. It must have been quite an ordeal for you.
Tony: It was hell. It was sheer hell down there. But I managed to keep things under control. Are the *Tonight* team here, *Panorama*, what about *Radio Newsreel*? I'm ready to give an interview. Where's the Scots bloke with the beard and the funny hat — what's his name, Heath Robertson?
Man: I'm afraid there's no one here, sir, but if you would all kindly follow me, the BBC would be delighted to give you all a cup of tea after your ordeal.
Tony: Very generous, I must say.
  (*They all follow the engineer down the stairs. Pause. Tony comes back. He goes into the lift and starts searching around. The lift attendant comes up and hangs an 'Out of Order' notice on the bell push. He sees Tony searching*)
Attendant: What are you looking for?
Tony: I've lost my season ticket. It must have fallen out of my pocket. I'm not paying one-and-nine when I've got a season ticket.
Attendant: Let's have a look.
  (*He joins Tony in the lift and starts searching on the floor with him. The doors close. The arrow over the lift starts going down and sticks between the same floors as before*)

154

SCENE 7   Inside the lift Tony is turning an imaginary camera.

Attendant: A film.
    (*Tony rings a bell, opens a book, and lights a candle, holds it up and walks round the lift with it*)
Attendant: *Bell, Book and Candle.*
Tony: Right first time, well done. Your go.
    (*Attendant pretends to sing*)
Tony: A song title.
Atttendant: Yes.
Tony: It's much better, just the two of us, isn't it? Go on. (*The attendant hops around in agony, mouthing 'Oh'*) Oh. (*Attendant touches the sole of his boot*) Shoe . . . sole. . . (*Attendant points to himself and mimes an Italian*) Me — Mio. 'O Sole Mio!' Very good. It's funny, I didn't like you at first. Funny how you can be wrong about people, isn't it?
Attendant: Your go.
Tony: Right. (*Cranks camera*) Tell me when you've had enough — we'll have a sing-song. . .

The Blood Donor

First transmitted on 23 June 1961

The Blood Donor featured
PATRICK CARGILL
HUGH LLOYD
JUNE WHITFIELD
FRANK THORNTON
JAMES OTTAWAY
PEGGYANN CLIFFORD
ANNE MARRYOTT
JEAN MARLOW

Produced by DUNCAN WOOD

SCENE 1 The Blood Donor Department of a large London hospital. There are several donors awaiting attention. A nurse is sitting at a reception desk. At the end of the room are some screens behind which the blood donations are taken. The waiting donors are reading magazines, etc. Tony enters. He goes up to the reception desk.

Nurse: Good afternoon, sir.

Tony: Good afternoon. I have come in answer to your advert on the wall next to the Eagle Laundry in Pelham Road.

Nurse: An advert? Pelham Road?

Tony: Yes. Your poster. You must have seen it. There's a nurse pointing at you, a Red Cross Lady actually, I believe, with a moustache and a beard — pencilled in, of course. You must know it, it's one of yours, next to Hands Off Cuba, just above the cricket stumps. It says 'Your Blood Can Save A Life'.

Nurse: Oh, I see, you wish to become a blood donor.

Tony: I certainly do. I've been thinking about this for a long time. Something for the benefit of the country as a whole. What should it be, I thought, become a blood donor or join the Young Conservatives? But as I'm not looking for a wife and I can't play table tennis, here I am. A bodyful of good British blood and raring to go. (*Rolls his sleeve up*)

Nurse: Yes, quite. Well, now, if you'd take a seat, I'll just take a few particulars.
    (*Tony sits down opposite her. He rolls his sleeve down. She takes a form and a pen*)

Nurse: Can I have your name?

Tony: Hancock. Anthony Hancock. Twice candidate for the County Council elections, defeated, Hon. Sec. British Legion, Earls Court Branch, Treasurer of the Darts Team and the Outings Committee.

Nurse: I only want the name.

Tony: We're going to Margate this year, by boat. If there are any young nurses like yourself who would care to join us, we would be more than happy to accommodate you.

Nurse: Thank you, I'll bear it in mind. Date of birth?

Tony: Er . . . yes. Shall we say the twelfth of May, nineteen — er — I always remember the twelfth of May, it was Coronation Day, you know — nineteen thirty-six.

Nurse: You're only twenty-five?

Tony: No, no, the Coronation was in 1936, I was born a little before that in — er — nineteen — er . . . (*makes a quick mental calculation*) Is all this really necessary?

Nurse: I'm afraid so. The twelfth of May. . . ?

Tony: Yes. I always remember that, the Coronation, we all got a day off at our school, did you? And we got a cup and saucer in a box and a bar of soap. Very good, I've still got that, and a spoon for the Silver Jubilee and a biscuit tin with their pictures on. . .

Nurse: How old are you?

Tony: (*disgruntled*) Thirty-five.

Nurse: Thank you. Nationality?

Tony: Ah, you've got nothing to worry about there. It's the blood you're thinking about, isn't it? British. Undiluted for twelve generations. One hundred per cent Anglo Saxon, with perhaps just a dash of the Viking, but nothing else has crept in. No, anybody who gets any of this will have nothing to complain about. There's aristocracy in there, you know. You want to watch who you're giving it to. It's like motor oil, it doesn't mix, if you get my meaning.

Nurse: Mr Hancock, when a blood transfusion is being given, the family background is of no consequence.

Tony: Oh, come now, surely you don't expect me to believe that. I mean after all east is east, really. . .

Nurse: (*slightly needled*) Mr Hancock, blood is blood the world over. It is classified by groups, not by accidents of birth.

Tony: I did not come here for a lecture on Communism, young lady.

Nurse: I happen to be a Conservative!

Tony: Then kindly behave like one, madam!

Nurse: Have you had any of these diseases?
(*She hands him a printed list. Tony reads it. He tries to remember a couple, looks uncomfortable at another one. Looks completely puzzled at another one*)

Tony: (*hands the list back*) No, I haven't. Especially that one. I've told you before, you have nothing to fear from me. I am perfectly healthy. Fit? Fit? If we'd had our own rocket, I could have been the first one up there. I had my name down for Blue Streak, but no, we missed our chance again. It's not right having these foreigners hurtling round up there, you mark my words. . .

Nurse: Mr Hancock —

Tony: Eh? Oh, I beg your pardon, I get carried away over things like that, it's a sore point with me. We ready now, then? (*He rolls up his sleeve again*)

Nurse: Just one more thing. Have you given any blood before?

Tony: Given, no. Spilt, yes. Yes, there's a good few drops lying about on the battlefields of Europe. Are you familiar with the Ardennes? I well remember Von Runstedt's last push — Tiger Harrison and myself, being in a forward position, were cut off behind the enemy lines. 'Captain Harrison,' I said. 'Yes, sir,' he said. 'Jerry's overlooked us,' I said, 'where shall we head for?' 'Berlin,' he said. 'Right,' I said, 'last one in the Reichstag is a cissy,' so we set off . . . got there three days before the Russians. . .

Nurse: You've never been a blood donor before?

Tony: No. So there we were, surrounded by Storm Troopers, 'Kamerad, Kamerad,' they said. . .

Nurse: (*has not taken any notice. Hands him a card*) If you will just sit over there with the others, Doctor will call you when he's ready.

Tony: Thank you. So we started rounding them up and. . .

(*Nurse gets up, puts some papers under her arm and leaves him*)

Tony: Oh.

(*He makes his way over to where the other donors are waiting their turn and sits down between two of them. He looks at the people round him*)

Tony: Well . . . it's a grand job we're all doing. (*Pause*) Yes, I think we can all be very proud of ourselves. Some people, all they do is take, take, take out of life, never put anything back. Well, that's not my way of living, never has been. You're only entitled to take out of life what you are prepared to put into it. (*Pause*) Do you get a badge for doing this?

Man: No, I don't think so.

Tony: Pity. We should have something for people to pick us out by.

Man: Surely, that's not the important thing. Just as long as we give the blood and help someone, that's the main thing.

Tony: Quite, quite — as long as they get their corpuscles, quite. That's reward in itself, I agree — no names, no pack drill, quite . . . I just think we ought to get a badge as well. I mean, nothing grand, a little enamelled thing, a little motto, that's all, nothing pretentious, 'He gaveth for others so that others may live' — I mean, we are do-gooders, we should get something for it.

Man: What do you want, money?

Tony: Don't be vulgar. I'm a great believer in charity. Help others, that's my motto. I contribute to every flag day that's going. The lapels of my suits are always the first thing to go. Covered in holes, they are. Yes, I always give what I can. (*Brings out his diary*) Here, you look at this, it's all in my diary. Congo Relief, two-and-six, Self-Denial Week, one-and-eight, Lifeboat Day, sixpence, Arab Refugees, one-and-two, it's all down here . . . yes . . . I do what I can. My conscience is clear. When I'm finally called by the Great Architect, and they say 'What did you do?' I'll just bring my book out, I'll say, 'Here you are, add that lot up.' I've got nothing to fear, I could go tomorrow. Ah yes. (*He puts the diary back and relaxes, very pleased with himself*) Do you come here often?

Man: This is my twelfth time.

Tony: Well, there's no need to boast about it, old man. How much did you give to the Arab Refugees?

Man: Oh, really.

Tony: No, come on, how much? You're shouting about how much blood you've given, how much did you give to the Arab Refugees?

Man: If you must know, I gave five pounds.

Tony: Oh. Well, some people are better placed than others.

Man: Well, let's forget about it, shall we?

Tony: Well, yes, all right.

2nd Nurse: (*comes to the door*) Mr Johnson — we're ready for you now.

Man: Yes, thank you.

(*The man gets up and goes into an annexe*)

Tony: (*to a large woman sitting on his other side*) A bit of a bighead, isn't he? If you can't give to charity without shouting about it from the rooftops — is this your first time?

Woman: I come here every six months, for the last twelve years.

Tony: Oh well, you've got a bit to spare, haven't you? Too much blood is as bad as too little, I always say.

Woman: Are you trying to be offensive?

Tony: No, no, nothing personal. Just an observation. I think it is very laudable to give so much. Of course, some people make it up quicker than others. I mean, I expect you're a big eater — it doesn't take you long to recoup the — er — that is to say — they've certainly brightened these hospitals up, haven't they? Of course, it's the Health Service that's done that. They spend more money on paint. Out of every thirteen-and-six paid in, sixpence ha'penny goes up on the wall. Well, it's worth it, I mean.

2nd Nurse: Mrs Forsythe, we're ready for you. Would you come this way?
(*The woman gets up and follows the nurse*)

Tony: (*calls after her*) Best of luck! Just think, Cliff Richard might get yours. (*To himself*) That'd slow him down a bit.
(*He settles back in his chair and looks around for something to do. Hums to himself. Crosses his legs. Bangs his knee with the side of his hand to make his leg jump up. It doesn't work. Bangs it harder. It still doesn't work. Bangs it quicker, hurts his knee and the side of his hand, but his knee still doesn't jump up. He stops doing it. A slight pause, and his knee jerks up. He looks puzzled at this. He takes his pulse. He can't find it. He feels all round his wrist — on the side of his temple — on the other wrist — he still can't find it. Puts his hand over his heart, smiles in relief as he feels it beating. Looks at the posters round the room*)

Tony: Drink-a pint-a milk-a day.
(*The reception desk nurse comes back and sits at her desk, a few yards away from Tony. He hasn't noticed her*)

Tony: (*recites*) Coughs and sneezes spread diseases. (*Sings to the tune of 'Deutschland über Alles'*) Coughs and sneezes spread diseases, trap the germs in your hand-kerchief, coughs and sneezes spread. . . (*He catches sight of the nurse, who is looking at him coldly. He smiles in embarrassment*) I — er — felt rather lonely sitting here by myself. It's funny what you do when you're on your own, isn't it? (*Laughs in embarrassment*) Is — er — is this a normal sort of day for you, then? Do you get many people in normally or is this — er — er — normal?

Nurse: (*without looking up from her work*) It's about average.

Tony: Yes, yes, quite. Yes indeed. My word, yes. (*Pause*) Of course, it's a vocation, nursing, I've always said that. One of the highest callings a woman can aspire to. (*Bored reaction from the nurse*) It's not the money, is it? Strange isn't it, the different values we place on society? I mean, you take modelling. You get some skinny bird, up in the West End, all bones and salt cellars, dragging a piece of fur along a platform — fifty quid a week. And there's you lot, dedicated, three years' training, humping great trolley loads of mince about all day long. It's not right. There's Adam Faith earning ten times as much as the Prime Minister. Is that right? Is that right? Mind you, I suppose it depends on whether you like Adam Faith and what your politics are.

(The nurse continues to work, not taking the slightest bit of notice)

Tony: I understand you get a cup of tea and a biscuit afterwards?

Nurse: Yes.

Tony: But no badge?

Nurse: No.

Tony: They're taking their time in there, aren't they? Everything's all right, I suppose?

Nurse: Yes.

Tony: Oh, I just wondered. I just thought some of the poor devils might pass out at the sight of a needle. I've seen it before. Men built like oak trees, keeling over like saplings in a hurricane. It was quite nasty.

Nurse: Needles don't bother you, then?

Tony: Me? No. I've had too many of them, my dear. I've had the lot. I've got arms like pin-cushions. Yes, I reckon I've had a syringeful of everything that's going in my time. Needles the size of drainpipes, some of them. You name it, I've had it.

(The second nurse comes out)

2nd Nurse: Mr Hancock, Doctor is ready for you now.

Tony: Who, me? Um . . . now? Yes, well . . . there's nobody else before me? I'm in no hurry. *(Looks round)* Does anybody want to go first?

2nd Nurse: There isn't anybody else, you're the last one.

Tony: Oh. Well . . . this is it, then. *(To the first nurse)* Here we go, then. Over the top. *(Confidentially, as they go into the annexe where the doctor is waiting)* What's he like on the needle, this bloke? Steady hand?

2nd Nurse: There's nothing to worry about.

Tony: Is he in a good mood?

2nd Nurse: You'll be quite all right. Doctor MacTaggart is an excellent doctor.

Tony: MacTaggart, he's a Scotsman? Ah well, that's all right. Marvellous doctors, the Scots, like their engineers, you know . . . first rate. It's the porridge, you know. Lead on, MacDuff.

    (*She leads him into the annexe where the doctor is sitting at a table. By him is all the paraphernalia required for blood donations*)

Tony: Ah, guid morning, it's a braw bricht moonlicht nicht the morning, mista, it's a bonny wee lassie ye got there helping you, hoots, the noo. . .

Doctor: (*educated English accent*) Would you mind sitting down there, Mr Hancock.

Tony: Oh. I beg your pardon for lapsing into the vernacular, but the young lady did say you were a Scottish gentleman.

Doctor: Yes, well, we're not all Rob Roys. May I have your card, please?

Tony: By all means. I'm ready when you are, squire.

    (*The doctor looks at the card*)

Doctor: Good. Nurse. (*The nurse brings a kidney bowl, a needle, a long thin tube*) Hold your hand out, please. (*Tony holds his hand out. The doctor takes the needle*) Now, this won't hurt. You'll just feel a slight prick on the end of your finger. (*Tony winces in readiness, eyes screwed shut. The doctor jabs the needle in*)

Tony: (*gets up as doctor smears the drop of blood from the needle on to a slide*) Well, I'll bid you good day, thank you very much, whenever you want any more, don't

hesitate to get in touch with me.

Doctor: Where are you going?

Tony: To have my tea and biscuits.

Doctor: I thought you came here to give some of your blood?

Tony: You've just had it.

Doctor: This is just a smear.

Tony: It may be just a smear to you, mate, but it's life and death to some poor wretch.

Doctor: No, no, no, I've just taken a small sample to test.

Tony: A sample? How much do you want then?

Doctor: Well, a pint, of course.

Tony: A pint? Have you gone raving mad? Oh, you must be joking.

Doctor: A pint is a perfectly normal quantity to take.

Tony: You don't seriously expect me to believe that? I came in here in all good faith to help my country. I don't mind giving a reasonable amount, but a pint — why, that's very nearly an armful. I don't mind that much (*holds out his finger*). But not up to here, mate, I'm sorry (*indicates just below his shoulder*). I'm not walking around with an empty arm for anybody. I mean, a joke's a joke. . .

Doctor: Mr Hancock, obviously you don't know very much about the workings of the human body. You won't have an empty arm, or an empty anything. The blood is circulating all the time. A normal healthy individual can give a pint of blood without any ill effects whatsoever. You do have eight pints of blood, you know.

Tony: Look, chum, everybody to his own trade, I'll grant you, but if I've got eight pints, obviously I need eight pints, and not seven, as I will have by the time you've finished with me. No, I'm sorry, I've been misinformed, I've made a mistake. I'll do something else, I'll be a traffic warden. . .

Doctor: Well, of course, I can't force you to donate your blood, but it's a great shame — you're AB Negative.

Tony: Is that bad?

Doctor: No, no, you're Rhesus-positive.

Tony: Rhesus? They're monkeys, aren't they? How dare you! What are you implying? I didn't come here to be insulted by a legalized vampire.

Doctor: Mr Hancock, that is your blood group. AB Negative. It is one of the rarest blood groups there is.

Tony: (*pleased*) Really?

Doctor: Yes, it is. Very rare indeed.

Tony: Oh. Well, of course, this does throw a different complexion on the matter. I mean, if I am one of the few sources, one doesn't like to hog it all, so to speak. I'm not un-Christian. Very rare, eh?

Doctor: I assure you there will be no ill effects, you'll make up the deficiency in no time at all.

Tony: Oh well, in that case, I'll do it. I mean, we AB Negatives must stick together. A minority group like us, we could be persecuted.

Doctor: Thank you very much, Mr Hancock, I'm most grateful. If you would go over to the bed and lie down, it won't take very long. Afterwards you rest for half an hour and then you're free to go.

(Tony lies down on the bed. The nurse wheels the blood-taking apparatus over. Tony watches apprehensively)
Doctor: Roll up your sleeve.
(Tony does so. The doctor starts preparing the apparatus. He dabs Tony's arm with cotton wool)
Tony: As a matter of interest, what group are you?
Doctor: Group A
Tony: *(disparagingly)* Huh.
Doctor: Now this won't hurt . . . relax. . .
(Tony tenses himself, relaxes at the command, then winces as the needle goes in, his face screwed up. He has a look down at his arm then turns his head away, feeling weak)

SCENE 2
A hospital room with several beds in it. All are occupied by blood donors, including the two Tony was speaking to earlier. Some are drinking tea. Tony is lying flat out on his bed. A little man is lying on the bed next to him.

Man: Are you all right?
Tony: Hmm? Oh yes, yes, fine. Nothing to it. What group are you?
Man: Group B. What group are you?
Tony: *(proudly)* AB Negative.
Man: Oh. That's very rare.
Tony: *(cocky)* I know. It's a funny thing, this blood business.
Man: Yes, I suppose it is.
Tony: It all looks the same and yet . . . it's all different. Yes, it's a very funny stuff, blood.
Man: Yes. I don't know where we'd be without it.
Tony: That's true. That's very true. Where would we be without it? Yes, it's very important, blood. It circulates right round the body, you know.
Man: Yes, so I believe.
Tony: Yes, it starts at the heart, it gets pumped right round, goes through the lungs, back into the heart, and round it goes again.
Man: What for?
Tony: What for? Well, it speaks for itself, doesn't it? I mean, the heart's got to have something to pump round . . . there's no point in it banging away all day long for no reason at all.
Man: Well, why have a heart, then?
Tony: Well, if you didn't, the blood wouldn't go round, would it? It'd all stay in one place. When you stood up, it'd all sink to the bottom of your legs. It'd be very uncomfortable, wouldn't it? It'd feel like you were walking around with a bootful of water. Your heart saves you keep having to stand on your head and jumping about to keep it moving. It does it for you.
Man: But I still don't see what good blood is, though.

Tony: Well . . . your body's full of veins, isn't it?

Man: Yes.

Tony: Well, you've got to fill them up with something, haven't you?

Man: Ah yes, I see. Are you a doctor, then?

Tony: Well, no, not really. I never really bothered.

Man: Oh.

Tony: Anything else troubling you? Any aches and pains?

Man: No, no. I'm all right.

Tony: Ah well, that's the main thing, isn't it? As long as you've got your health.

Man: Nothing else matters really, does it?

Tony: No. And the funny thing is, you know, you never appreciate it until you haven't got it any more.

Man: Yes. Some people take their health for granted, don't they?

Tony: Do you know, that could have been me talking. You took the words right out of my mouth. Yes, if you haven't got your health, you haven't got anything.

Man: Mind you, they do some marvellous things these days.

Tony: Oh yes, it's advanced a lot, medical science. I'm glad they slung away the leeches. That was the turning point. I mean, look at the things they can do these days. New blood, plastic bones, false teeth, glasses, wigs . . . Do you know, there's some people walking around with hardly anything they started out with.

Man: Yes, what would we do without doctors, eh?

Tony: (*making a point*) Or, conversely, what would *they* do without *us*?

Man: That's true. That's very shrewd.

Tony: But the main thing is, look after yourself.

Man: You look after your body and your body will look after you.

Tony: That's very wise. Of course, the Greeks, they knew all this years ago.

Man: Did they really?

Tony: Oh yes, very advanced people, the Greeks were. They had hot and cold water and drains, always washing themselves, they were. Of course, it all got lost in the wars.

Man: When Mussolini moved in.

Tony: No, no, before him. They taught it to the Romans, then the Romans came over here. . .

Man: Well, of course, you can always learn from other people.

Tony: Of course you can. That's why I'm in favour of the Common Market. You can't ignore the rest of the world.

Man: That's true. That's very true.

Tony: You can't go through life with your head buried in the sand.

Man: No man is an island.

Tony: You're right. There I agree, Necessity is the mother of invention.

Man: It certainly is. Life would be intolerable if we knew everything.

Tony: I should say it would. My goodness, yes. Let the shipwrecks of others be your sea marks.

Man: For things unknown there is no desire.

Tony: Well, exactly. And then again, a bird in the hand is worth two in the bush.

Man: It is indeed.

Tony: Do you like winegums?

Man: Thank you very much.

Tony: Don't take the black one.

Man: No, all right. Of course, they do a tube with all black ones now, you know.

Tony: I know, but you can't always get them.

Man: Well, that's the way it goes.

Tony: Still, as long as we've got our health.

Man: Yes, that's the main thing.

Tony: Yes, that's the main thing. Ah, yes. Yes, indeed.

Man: Well, I think I'm ready now.

Tony: Oh, you're off, then?

Man: Yes, out into the big world.

Tony: Do you live far?

Man: Just up the road.

Tony: You'll get a bus, then, will you?

Man: No, I think I'll walk.

Tony: You haven't got far to go, then?

Man: No, just up the road.

Tony: Oh, well, it's not worth it, then, is it?

Man: No, not really.

Tony: Oh, well, I'll say cheerio, then.

Man: Yes, cheerio. Look after yourself.

Tony: Yes, and you.

Man: I will.

Tony: Don't do anything I wouldn't do, will you? (*Laughs*)

Man: I won't. Well, cheerio, then.

Tony: Cheerio.

    (*The man leaves*)

Tony: A nice man that, a very nice man. Very intelligent. Good conversationalist. A cut above the type you meet down the pub. A very nice man. (*Feels in his pocket*) He's walked off with my wine gums! I only broke them open for him. Oh, what's the use, if you can't trust blood donors who can you trust? (*Calls*) Nurse, what about some tea down here? You've had my blood, it's not asking for much is it, really? And two spoonfuls of brown sugar . . . Dear oh dear. . .

★ ★ ★

SCENE 3   Tony's sitting-room. He is dialling on the phone.

Tony: Hallo, South London Hospital? Doctor MacTaggart, please. Blood Donor Department. (*Hums to himself*) Hallo, doctor, Hancock here. Yes, it is me again. Has it gone yet? Have you used it? My blood. You've had it twenty-four hours now, you said it was rare, surely someone must be after it? Well, of course it's got something to do with me. It's my blood. Yes, all right, *was*. But you can't expect my interest in it to cease just because you've got it. It's a waste of time giving it if it's just going to lie about in a bottle for years. I wish to make sure it goes to the right sort of person. I wouldn't like to think of any old hobbledehoy having my blood coursing through his veins . . . Well, really, I never thought I'd hear that sort of language from a doctor. Have you been at the methylated spirits? Control yourself, sir, there might be nurses listening. Civility costs nothing, my man. I will phone when I like. I will phone tomorrow, and the day after, and the day after that, and everyday until my blood is used. Good day to you. (*He puts the receiver down*) What a way to speak to a blood donor. (*He goes into the kitchen to cut some bread*) If I have any more of his old buck I shall go straight to the Hospital Management Committee, have his licence taken away. I think it's reasonable to want to know where your life's blood has gone to. Especially a rare group like mine.

(*As he speaks he is having difficulty in cutting the loaf. He takes a sharpener and starts sharpening the knife*)

★ ★ ★

IRELAND

SCENE 4

The Casualty Ward. Tony is lying on a stretcher, wrapped in blankets, with his hand swathed in bandages and a tourniquet on his arm. A doctor comes in and takes Tony's report card from a nurse.

Doctor: Knife wound, eh? Teddy boy, is he?

Nurse: No, I don't think so. His landlady found him. Cut himself with a bread knife and fainted.

Doctor: Lost a lot of blood, I see.

Nurse: Yes.

Doctor: We'll have to give him a transfusion.

Nurse: He had his blood donor's card on him. He's group AB Negative.

Doctor: Really? That's very rare. Have we got any?

Nurse: I've checked, and we've got just one pint in stock.

Doctor: Good. Get it, will you, nurse? (*He goes over to Tony*) You're going to be all right, old man. We're going to give you a transfusion.

Tony: (*weakly*) I'm a very rare blood group, you know.

Doctor: Yes, we know. We've got just one pint of your group in stock, we're going to give that to you.

(*Dr MacTaggart enters, carrying the blood*)

MacTaggart: Who wants the pint of AB Negative? (*He sees Tony*) Oh no — it's not for him? He only gave it yesterday. (*To Tony*) Waste of time, wasn't it?

Tony: Well, I'd have been in a right state if I hadn't — there's nothing else here for me. At least I know it's going to the right sort of person. These blood banks are just like ordinary banks, really — put it in when you're flush, draw it out when you need it. Come on, bang it in, I'm getting dizzy. I'll let you have it back later on. Do you get tea and biscuits after getting blood as well? What's on the menu tonight?